A taste of New Brunswick

Recipes from our kitchens

by Karen Elaine Powell

Edited by Susan Flood

Neptune Publishing Company Ltd.

A taste of New Brunswick

A Taste of New Brunswick !
Copyright © 2001 – Karen Elaine Powell
Neptune Publishing Company Ltd.
Printed in Canada 10 9 8 7 6 5
Design & Typesetting – Paul Evans, Evans Communications Inc.
Editor – Susan Flood
Cover Photo – Rob Roy Reproductions

The publisher wishes to acknowledge and thank the department of Municipalities, Culture and Housing for their assistance in this publication.

Canadian Cataloguing in Publication Data
ISBN 1-896270-17-4
Powell, Karen Elaine, 1967-
A Taste of New Brunswick !
1.Cookery, Canadian-New Brunswick style. I. Title.
TX715.6.P692001 641.59715 C2001-901137-7

Sections

Acknowledgement

I wish to thank the staff of Neptune Publishing.

The friends who helped with research
and spent endless hours with me
tasting and experimenting.

My co-workers over the past few years
who have tried and tested many of these recipes,
offering words of praise.

I hope many more people
will now be able to enjoy some
of these delicious New Brunswick treasures.

How to use this book

A recipe is just a guide for cooking, and is not written in stone. Start out by reading a recipe to be certain that you like all of the ingredients and that the ingredients are stocked in your pantry. Get all of the ingredients ready, vegetables cleaned and cut up, cooking utensils ready, herbs and spices measured out and any special tools or dishes ready. Always have your cooking surface pre-lined or pre-greased if needed. Everything should be on hand before you start to cook.

It may happen that there is a spice, herb, cheese or meat that is not your favorite listed in a recipe. Just replace it with the food of your choice that is of similar texture and consistency.

Food is best when it is fresh, so always use the freshest vegetables, fish, meat and herbs. Be careful not to leave perishable food out too long. Use clean kitchen manners to keep food fresh and to abolish any chance of food poisoning.

Some recipes can be adjusted to be fat free or low in fat, but some just don't taste the same without that heavy cream or that extra tablespoon of butter. If that is the case then choose another recipe to try if you are watching your fat intake.

All of my recipes are in regular cups and pound measurements. For those who prefer to use metric measurements, there is a page of conversion at the end of this book.

New Brunswick

New Brunswick is a scenic place to visit.

It covers 73,440 sq.km or 28,354 sq.mi and 85% of it is forested. The unpopulated area is amazing to the big city dweller.

◀ Its' capital city is Fredericton.

Summers are warm but not too hot. Temperatures are much cooler along the coast.

The provincial flag is a gold lion on a red ▶ compartment with an ancient oared gallery.

The flower of the province was chosen in 1936. It is the ◀ purple violet.

The chickadee was named the provincial bird ▶ in 1983.

◀ The New Brunswick tartan was designed by the late Miss Patricia Jenkins and has been used since 1959. It reflects the colors of the forest in the fall.

New Brunswick is Canada's only officially bilingual province.

English *Anglais*
Français *French*

The time zone in New Brunswick is Atlantic Daylight Time.

◀ New Brunswick boasts many historical sites. One being the Hartland Covered Bridge. This is the longest covered bridge in the world. It is man made and measures 390 meters or 1282 feet.

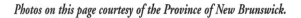

Photos on this page courtesy of the Province of New Brunswick.

Sides, Soups & Such

Gravy

1. Gravy is made from the drippings from meat combined with the cooking liquid from vegetables. Some stock or water may be added to produce the volume of gravy needed. Avoid adding too much liquid to the meat drippings as the flavor will be too diluted. Then the liquid is thickened by various methods.

2. Add spices such as parsley, garlic, mint, basil, soya sauce, or worcestershire sauce to flavor the gravy. For additional flavor, boil 1/2 lb. of meat in 2 cups of water or stock until cooked. Then purée the meat with 1/4 cup onion, and 1/4 cup celery. Add this to the gravy.

3. Commercial gravy browning may be added to darken the gravy. Bring the gravy to a boil, then turn the heat back so it is just under a boil. Do not add the thickener when liquid is boiling as this will cook the thickener into lumps. Add thickener little by little, stirring constantly until desired thickness is reached. Reduce heat once it starts to thicken.

4. "Au jus" gravy is a thin liquid form of gravy that does not contain the juice from any vegetables. It is only the drippings from the meat that has been reduced by cooking until it thickens naturally. This produces a stronger flavor.

Winter Corn Chowder

This heart warming soup combined with a green salad and crusty bread makes a filling main dish.

2 cups	potatoes cubed
1/2 cup	onion minced
2 cups	evaporated milk
1 cup	cream of chicken soup
3 cups	vegetable or chicken stock
1 tbsp.	garlic minced
1/2 cup	celery diced
1/2 cup	green pepper diced
3 cups	corn (whole or cream)
1 tbsp.	soya sauce
1 tsp.	white pepper
2 tbsp.	butter
Salt & pepper to taste.	

1. In a large pot, brown the onion, garlic in butter until golden brown in color.

2. Add all the rest of the ingredients and cook over low heat for 1 hour until potatoes are tender. Serve piping hot!

Smooth & Creamy Tomato Soup

New Brunswick's coastal climate keeps the temperature in winter, spring and fall ideal for cooking up a big pot of soup. Everybody seems to be gardening these days. Here's a recipe to use up some of this years' bumper crop of tomatoes.

1/2 cup	onion minced
1 tbsp.	butter
1/2 cup	celery minced
3 cups	tomatoes chopped, fresh or canned
1 cup	tomato paste
1 tbsp.	garlic minced
1 tbsp.	parsley
1 tsp.	white pepper
1/4 cup	basil (dried)
1	bay leaf
1 cup	evaporated milk
2 cups	chicken stock
1 tbsp.	white sugar
1/2 cup	sour cream
1 tbsp.	soya sauce
1 tbsp.	worcestershire sauce

Salt to taste.

1. Fry the onion, garlic, celery, spices, and tomatoes in butter until the onion is transparent.

2. Place all in a deep pot, and add the rest of the ingredients.

3. Simmer 1 hour on low.

Creamy Garlic Salad Dressing

2 cups	mayonnaise
1 cup	olive oil
2/3 cup	white vinegar
1/4 cup	lemon juice
3 tbsp.	garlic minced or 1 tsp. powder
2 tbsp.	oregano
Salt & pepper to taste.	

1. Blend all of the ingredients until smooth, about 5 minutes by hand.

2. Let sit overnight before using to allow for the flavor to blend and strengthen.

Tip: If you use garlic powder the mixture will last longer and be stronger in flavor as powder is more concentrated. Shake the dressing well before using if made with garlic powder.

Hint: This mixture will last approximately 3 weeks in the refrigerator. Makes approximately 1 litre of dressing.

Hint: This is a wonderful creamy dressing for salads, a delicious dipping sauce for vegetables and a great sauce for a meat dish.

Spiced Rice

This dish will liven up a meal of baked fish, adding a bit of color to the plate as well.

4 cups	rice cooked
1 cup	mushrooms sliced
1 cup	onion minced
1 cup	green pepper minced
1/4 cup	almonds slivered
1/2 tsp.	chili powder
1 tsp.	garlic minced
1 tbsp.	butter
1 tsp.	cayenne pepper
Salt & pepper to taste.	

1. Sauté cayenne, chili, vegetables, and almonds in butter.

2. Once all is cooked, add rice and stir until evenly mixed.

Spinach & Feta in Filo with Mushrooms

1 cup	uncooked spinach, minced per person
1/2 cup	mushrooms, minced per person
1/4 cup	feta cheese crumbled per person
2 sheets	filo pastry per person
2 tbsp.	melted butter
Salt & pepper to taste.	

1. Mix spinach, feta, mushrooms, salt & pepper well in a small bowl. Set aside.

2. Lay the 2 sheets of filo on top of each other and brush with melted butter. Spread the spinach mixture on the filo pastry, and roll up the sheets like a log.

3. Brush with melted butter, then bake on a cookie sheet at 350 ° F for 20 minutes until the pastry is golden brown.

Vegetable Beef Soup

1 lb.	steak cut into bite size pieces
1 cup	onion diced
1 tsp.	garlic minced
1 tbsp.	soya sauce
1/2 tsp.	mint
4 cups	beef stock
1 cup	crushed tomatoes
1 tbsp.	basil
1 cup	mushrooms sliced
1 cup	carrots diced
1/2 cup	celery diced
1 tbsp.	olive oil
Salt & pepper to taste.	

1. Brown meat in frying pan with 1 tbsp. of olive oil.

2. Reduce heat and add garlic, basil and mint. Fry just another minute to a
   vate the herbs.

3. In a large pot combine all ingredients with meat mixture. Let simmer 1/2
   hour, stirring occasionally over medium heat. Be sure to keep the liquid a
   least two inches above the vegetables at all times. This may mean adding
   stock as the vegetables absorb liquid as they cook. Simmer on low heat fo
   1/2 hour.

Homemade Chicken Vegetable Soup

n our parents day, nothing was wasted. Leftovers from a chicken would be sed to create a delicious broth. This recipe skips that step but still produces a up you could even serve your mother.

large	chicken breasts, raw boneless, skinless & diced
cups	chicken broth
cup	onion diced
cups	carrot diced
cup	mushroom sliced
cup	celery diced
tsp.	garlic minced
tsp.	white pepper
tbsp.	soya sauce
/4 tsp.	dill
/2 cup	green peas
tsp.	parsley
/2 cup	rice (optional) *

. Place all ingredients into a large deep pot and bring to a boil.

. Reduce heat and simmer for 1 hour on low. Serve.

* * *

ravel back to the 19th Century at Kings Landing Historical Settlement in rince William. The "residents" dressed in authentic costumes give a glimpse nto the daily lives of our forefathers. You can even try some of the original ecipes from the region in the local inn.

Yorkshire Pudding

1 cup	flour
1 tsp.	salt
1 cup	milk
2	eggs
1/4 tsp.	garlic powder
1 tbsp.	soya sauce
1 tbsp.	worcestershire sauce
Pepper to taste.	

1. Place all of the above ingredients into a deep bowl.

2. Mix all well until smooth. Place in refrigerator covered.

3. Use in a 9" x 13" pan or muffin tin, lightly greased, pour 1/2 cup meat drippings. Place in a 400° F oven until pan is hot.

4. Remove pan from oven, add mixture to pan. Return to oven for 1/2 hour.

Hint: You can make this mixture the night before and keep it in the fridge overnight. This allows for the mixture to bind, thus producing a fluffier bread.

* * *

New Brunswickers particularly in the South, are proud of their British Loyalist heritage. In 1783, 14,000 Loyalists arrived in New Brunswick, landing at the mouth of the St. John River and swelling the population of what is now called Saint John.

Herbed Churned Butter

2 cups	butter

1. Whip the butter for 2 minutes. Add one or more of the below seasonings and beat again for 1 minute.

Seasonings:

2 tbsps.	parsley
2 tbsps.	garlic minced plus 1 tbsp. parsley
2 tbsps.	mint
2 tbsps.	basil
2 tbsps.	rosemary
1 tsp.	coriander
1 tsp.	Cinnamon
2 tsp.	cayenne pepper
2 tsp.	chili powder
1/2 cup	crushed berries such as cranberries, or even blueberries.

Hint: Serve as a spread for toast, or for frying or basting.

Tangy & Tart Mustard Dressing

1 cup	mustard
1/2 cup	vegetable oil
1 cup	red wine vinegar
1/4 cup	lemon juice
1 tsp.	pepper
1 tsp.	garlic minced
1 tsp.	oregano
1 tsp.	soya sauce

1. Mix all of the ingredients in a bowl until evenly distributed, about 5 minutes by hand.

Serve with a garden salad or use it as a sauce for baking chicken, pork, ham or beef in.

Vinegar Dressing

1 cup	vegetable oil
1 cup	vinegar (red or white)
1/4 cup	lemon juice
1 tbsp.	parsley
1/4 tsp.	pepper
1 tsp.	garlic minced
1/4 tsp.	oregano

1. Mix all of the above ingredients well, store in the fridge in an airtight container. Serve over any type of tossed salad.

Cajun Hot Vinegar Dressing

4 cups	red wine vinegar
1/2 cup	black peppercorns crushed
1 cup	jalapeno peppers sliced
1/4 cup	garlic minced

1. Bring all of the ingredients to a boil. Let boil for 10 minutes over medium heat. Cool, and strain.

2. Bottle the clear liquid by placing a double layer of cheese cloth in a strainer, pour the mixture through. This will collect all the peppercorns and peppers .

Fundy Fog Pea Soup

This soup is a staple in Maritime Kitchens.

2 cups	split peas (green or yellow) uncooked
3/4 cup	onion minced
6 cups	water or chicken stock
1 tbsp.	soya sauce
1 cup	ham pieces, & ham bone if available
Salt & pepper to taste.	
Dumplings (optional)*	

1. Simmer over low to medium heat until all peas are dissolved. Approximately 2 hours.

2. If you like a full bodied soup you can add diced carrot, turnip or even potatoes. About 1 cup of each would be good for the final hour of cooking time.

3. Serve piping hot.

It is a traditional favorite for a wintery Saturday supper after an afternoon on the frozen river.

* Dumplings may be cooked in the soup, during the last 20-30 minutes of cooking time before serving.

* * *

Work up an appetite at Fundy National Park. With 100 kilometres / 60 miles of walking trails and fabulous scenery it is a jewel in New Brunswick's crown of wonderful holiday destinations. The Bay of Fundy boasts the world's highest tides.

Fresh Avocado Dressing

4	regular sized avocados ripe
1/2 cup	olive oil
1 tbsp.	garlic minced
1 tsp.	pepper
1/2 tsp.	salt
1 cup	plain yogurt
1/2 tsp.	basil
1 tsp.	mustard
2 tbsp.	tomato paste

1. Place all of the above ingredients in a food processor or blender and purée until smooth.

2. Remove and stir to make sure it is evenly blended.

3. Prepare vegetables for dipping such as carrot sticks, celery sticks, cherry tomatoes, broccoli, etc…

4. Bottle the sauce in an air tight container. It will keep 2 weeks in the refrigerator.

Hint: Serve as a dressing for salad or use it for a vegetable dip.

* * *

The power of the Fundy tides is the most dramatically displayed by the unique rock formations at Hopewell Cape. These four storey rock formations have been carved into the shape of flowerpots by the pounding surf.

Pasta Salad with Garden Fresh Tomato Dressing

1 cup	yogurt or soft cheese like ricotta or cottage
1 cup	tomato juice
1 tbsp.	garlic minced
1 tsp.	oregano
1 tsp.	basil
1 tsp.	pepper
1 tsp.	salt
1/4 cup	olive oil
4 cups	small pasta shells, cooked

1. In a deep bowl mix all of the ingredients until smooth, by hand for about 7 minutes.

2. Refrigerate overnight before using. This allows the flavors to develop.

3. Shake before using. To thicken if necessary add 1 tbsp. tomato paste and stir.

4. Serve as a dressing for a pasta salad or greens, or use as a sauce for baking meat or vegetables with.

* * *

Pack the pasta in the cooler with some thirst quenching apple cider and some fresh buns from the market. Now you're set for a picnic at the park. Fundy National Park has scenic hiking trails for all levels of ability in addition to fabulous picnic sights.

Hearty & Hot Tomato Soup

The horseradish in this soup gives it quite a bite. Enjoy it with a salad of fresh greens.

4 cups	beef broth
1 cup	horseradish minced
1 tbsp.	garlic minced
1 tbsp.	basil
3 cups	crushed tomatoes
1 can	evaporated milk
1/2 cup	tomato paste

Salt & pepper to taste.

1. Place all of the ingredients except the milk into a large pot and simmer for 1 hour over low heat. Add milk and simmer 20 minutes longer.

Mustard Sauce

This versatile sauce can be used as a dipping sauce for vegetables, hors d'oeuvres or as a sauce for cooking fish or meat.

1 cup	mustard
1 cup	cold béchamel sauce *
or	1 cup sour cream
or	1 cup ricotta
1/4 cup	lemon juice
1 tsp.	oil
1 tsp.	garlic minced
1 tsp.	lemon or orange zest
1 spring	parsley fresh

Salt & pepper to taste.

1. Mix all except parsley well in a large deep bowl until smooth. Garnish with parsley. Will last one week in refrigerator.

* Recipe for béchamel sauce on page 75.

Turkey, Mushroom & Mozzarella Melt

This sandwich is made like a traditional grilled cheese.

2 slices	bread
1 tbsp.	garlic butter
3 oz	turkey sliced
1/4 cup	mushrooms sliced & sautéed
1 tsp.	onion minced
2 tsp.	ranch salad dressing
1/4 cup	mozzarella shredded
Salt & pepper to taste.	

1. Butter the outsides of both slices of bread with the garlic butter and lay one buttered side down into a frying pan. Butter the inside of the slices of bread with 1 tsp. of ranch dressing.

2. Layer on the turkey, mushrooms, onion and cheese.

3. Place the 2nd slice of bread on top of sandwich to close. Cover the frying pan to keep the heat in so all the insides of the sandwich get a chance to warm up.

4. Cook over medium heat until 1st side becomes crispy.

Flip to crisp the other side.

* * *

The Fundy Trail Parkway follows the coast of the Bay of Fundy from St. Martins to Big Salmon River. It is accessible to hikers and motorists alike. Start your trip with a visit to the sea caves at St. Martins.

Summertime Raspberry Vinaigrette

4 cups	white wine vinegar
2 cups	fresh or frozen raspberries
1	grated rind of whole lemon
1 tsp.	black peppercorns whole

1. Bring all of the above ingredients to a boil. Let boil for 10 minutes over medium heat.

2. Cool, strain and bottle.

3. Strain by placing a double layer of cheese cloth in a strainer.

Pour the mixture through. This will collect all the loose particles to produce a clear liquid.

4. Bottle in an airtight container, keep refrigerated.

Hint: Serve over salad, or in place of vinegar in another recipe.

* * *

Sussex is in the heart of Kings County; catch the Atlantic Balloon Fiesta in September where you will see as many as 25 hot air balloons take flight to the skies. While in Kings County be sure to see some of the covered bridges still in use today.

Thickening

Cornstarch & Water method

1. The mixture must be made with cold water as warm water will cook the starch, turning it into glue. You must also add the water to the cornstarch otherwise it will clump. The mixture should be as thick as corn syrup when ready. A large amount would never exceed 3/4 cup of cornstarch powder. For smaller dishes such as a sauce usually 2 - 3 tsps. of cornstarch will do. This method is used for one time meals as it does not reheat well. Once reheated it appears to be jellied and lumpy and will not smooth out completely. Usually because this thickener has a glossy appearance, many cooks prefer it for their sauces and Stir-fry. You can keep any excess liquid in a sealed jar in the fridge for 3 weeks.

2. Bring the liquid that you want to thicken to a boil and then turn back the heat to just under boiling and add the thickener bit by bit, while stirring constantly. The liquid will thicken. If the desired thickness has not occurred, add more thickener. Reduce heat until ready to use.

Flour & Water method

1. This mixture has the same properties as the cornstarch mixture. The mixture must be made with cold water, and the water must be added to the flour. First you bring liquid to boil, reduce it, and then thicken (same as cornstarch method).

2. For this method you will need at least 1 cup flour to about 2 cups water ratio. Place flour in a tight lidded container, add water and shake well. Open and see if it is too thick or too thin. It should be about as thick as honey. This method if you use too much will have a flour taste to your sauce. Bring liquid to a boil, reduce, thicken and stir.

Rue method

1. This method is totally different. You melt 1/2 cup of butter on low heat and add flour to it until all the butter is absorbed and the mixture is dry and crumbly, about 3/4 to 1 cup of flour.

2. Remove from heat and let cool, if you want you can store it or you can use it right away if needed. It will store in the fridge for 3 weeks in a sealed jar. It is mainly used for large portions of soups , chowders or clear sauces . You can also use it in smaller things like sauces and gravy. Any dish using this method re-heats well.

3. When ready to use , simply add some to whatever you want to thicken and keep stirring, the mixture will dissolve and thicken your dish.

Reducing method

1. Instead of adding a thickener, this method subtracts liquid. You are basically dehydrating a dish when you reduce. If the liquid contains pieces of meat you may want to remove meat so as not to toughen it by the quick high heat.

2. Bring the liquid to a rapid boil on high heat and be careful not to burn it until part of the liquid has evaporated. Typically the liquid is reduced by 1/3. Then return your meat to the dish to reheat it and then toss with the sauce.

Coating food method

1. You can coat food with cornstarch or flour and then brown it in a frying pan with a little oil or butter and then cook your recipe as normal. Then when you add liquid to your dish, the flour/cornstarch will thicken the dish a little. If you are baking the dish, it usually thickens just a bit more.

Spring Time
Tomato Basil Soup

This is the perfect lunch after a morning spent in the garden. If you still have some tomatoes preserved from last years bounty, use them to remind you of what is to come.

1 cup	onion diced
1 cup	mushrooms sliced
1 cup	celery diced
1 cup	green pepper diced
1 cup	carrots diced
2 tbsp.	basil
1 tsp.	white pepper
1 tsp.	oregano
1 tbsp.	garlic minced
3 cups	crushed tomatoes
1 cup	tomato paste
3-5 cups	stock
Salt to taste.	

1. Place all of the ingredients in a large deep pot. Add enough stock to cover vegetables with two inches of stock.

2. Simmer 1 hour on low heat stirring occasionally. Serve.

* * *

Gardeners' and lovers of flowers and fauna will love to stroll through the Kingsbrae Gardens in St. Andrews. The 27 acres offer something for everyone from roses to heathers to butterfly bushes. It is awesome.

Hot Pepper Relish

10	jalapeno peppers
4	green chili peppers
1	red chili pepper
1 tsp.	crushed chilies
2 tbsps.	lemon juice
1/4 cup	garlic minced
1/4 tsp.	salt
1 tbsp.	white sugar

1. Be careful of the fumes and juices from the peppers. Do not touch any skin or inhale fumes as this may burn.

2. Place all of the above into the blender or food processor and purée until loosely chunked.

3. Store in the refrigerator in an airtight container. Lasts 3 weeks.

Avocado Sandwich

1/2	avocado sliced thin
1/4 cup	alpha sprouts
1/2	tomato sliced thin
1 slice	swiss cheese
2 slices	multi grain or cracked wheat bread

Salt & pepper to taste.

1. Toast bread lightly.

2. Layer ingredients on one slice of toast as follows: avocado, salt & pepper, sprouts, and cheese.

3. Place the sandwich on a cookie sheet and place under broiler in oven to melt cheese. Top with the other slice of toast.

Onion Dip

1 cup	sour cream
1/4 cup	green onion chopped
1 tbsp.	parsley
1/4 cup	onion minced
1 tsp.	garlic minced
1 tbsp.	soya sauce
1 tbsp.	worcestershire sauce
1/2 envelope	commercial dry onion soup mix powder

1. Mix all of the above ingredients in a bowl until evenly blended.

2. Place in a decorative serving dish and cover tightly and store in fridge for 4 hours before serving. This allows the flavors to develop.

Hint: Great for chip dip, vegetable dip, salad dressing or as a spread for sandwiches.

Spiced Nut Spread

2 cups	chick peas, canned (juice reserved)
1 tsp.	white pepper
Salt	to taste
1/4 cup	lemon juice
1 tbsp.	soya sauce
1 cup	tahini sauce
1/4 cup	garlic minced
1/2 cup	sesame seeds toasted

1. Place all into a food processor and purée.

2. Add the juice from chick peas slowly until desired thinness is reached. Keep refrigerated.

3. Serve as a dip or spread on toast or pita bread.

Cheese Ball

1 cup	cream cheese (softened)
1 cup	old cheddar grated
1 cup	havarti grated
1/4 cup	parmesan cheese freshly grated
1 tsp.	fresh chives or green onion chopped
1 tsp.	garlic minced
1 tsp.	cracked black peppercorns
dash	salt
1 tsp.	worcestershire sauce
1 cup	crushed mixture*

1. Mix in blender or food processor.

2. Form into a log or ball shape and chill for 2 hours until firm.

3. Brush the outside with 2 tbsp. corn or maple syrup.

4. Roll cheese shape in a crushed mixture, reshape and chill.

5. *Crushed mixture can be a combination of nuts, cereal and/or herbs, eg. pecans, walnuts, cashews, almonds, brazil, bran or cornflakes.

6. Cool until ready to use and then let it sit at room temperature for 30 minutes before serving. Serve with assorted crackers, biscuits, crispy bread and firm vegetables.

Try adding parsley, thyme, mint, basil or even minced vegetables like broccoli, red and green peppers or onions for appearance.

Garden Fresh French Onion Soup

4 cups	onions sliced in rounds
1/4 cup	garlic minced
1 tbsp.	clarified butter
1 tbsp.	parsley
4 cups	beef broth *
1 cup	water
1 cup	chicken stock
4 slices	bread
1/2 cup	finely shredded soft cheese per person, mozzarella or swiss
Salt & pepper to taste.	

Hot peppers or green tomatoes can be added for a different touch.

1. Sauté onions and garlic in butter until onions are caramelized.

2. Add beef, chicken broth, water, parsley, and salt & pepper.

4. Boil gently for 10 minutes, and then simmer for 10 minutes on low heat.

5. Toast a slice of bread till it is really dry. A slice of garlic bread works well.

6. Place bread on top of bowl of soup. Top bread with 1/4 cup of cheese. Place one small scoopful of soup on top to melt cheese. Then add the other 1/4 cup of cheese on top. Bread will slowly sink into the soup.

* Hint: You can use drippings or even some gravy from a roast of beef dinner for added flavor.

Potato Salad

New Brunswickers love picnics and potlucks. This salad travels well to either. It will feed 15 people as a side dish.

5 lbs.	potatoes, cooked, cooled & mashed
2 cups	canned mixed green peas and carrots
1 apple	diced small
1 cup	corn fresh or canned
1/2 cup	onion minced
1/2 cup	celery minced
1 tsp.	garlic minced
6 eggs	hard boiled & mashed
1 cup	mayonnaise
1/2 cup	ranch salad dressing
Salt & pepper to taste.	

1. Mix eggs, mayonnaise, and ranch dressing together and add to the mashed potatoes. Stir well until all is evenly mixed.

2. Add the harder vegetables, apple, corn, onion, celery, and garlic into the potatoes and stir again until evenly mixed.

3. Fold in the mixed carrots and peas.

4. Place into a casserole dish, garnish and cool in the fridge till ready to use.

Honeyed
Fruit & Vegetable Dip

1 cup	yogurt
1/2 cup	honey
Cinnamon	to taste

1. Blend well. (about 5 minutes by hand).

2. Serve with a variety of sliced fruits and vegetables.

Sweet Fruit Dip

1 cup	yogurt any flavor
1 cup	sour cream
1 cup	marshmallow topping eg. Fluff

1. Mix all until even (about 5 minutes by hand).

2. Chill for 2 hours before serving.

* * *

New Brunswick boasts a 1000 kilometer / 600 mile trail system with a wealth of unspoiled beauty to behold. It includes a section of the Trans-Canada Trail which will become the longest trail on earth.

Home-style Pumpkin Soup

Served hot or cold, this is a delicious way to decorate your Thanksgiving table.

1 medium	pumpkin
4 cups	canned soft pumpkin
1/2 cup	onion minced
2 tbsp.	garlic minced
1 tbsp.	butter
1 pear	peeled, sliced thin & minced
2 cups	chicken stock
1 cup	evaporated milk
1 cup	whipping cream
1/2 cup	sour cream
1 tsp.	thyme
1/2 tsp.	cumin
Dash	cinnamon
Salt & pepper to taste.	

1. Remove seeds from pumpkin.

2. In a hot frying pan sauté over medium heat the onion and garlic in the butter until onion is tender and golden.

3. In a large stock pot place sautéed vegetables, pumpkin, pear, chicken stock, thyme, and cumin. Stir well.

4. Simmer 20 minutes over medium heat, stirring often. Add all of the rest of ingredients and simmer on low heat stirring often for 30 minutes.

5. Whisk with electric mixer for 3 minutes before serving to fluff the whipping cream and produce a light airy soup.

6. Serve in the empty pumpkin shell that has been warmed in the oven for 20 minutes on 250° F.

Garden Salad Croutons

1/4 cup	oil
1 tbsp.	garlic powder
1 tsp.	basil
1/2 tsp.	chili powder
1 tsp.	oregano
1 tsp.	parsley
3 cups	bread cubed
Salt & pepper to taste.	

1. Use any type of bread, cut into cubes.

2. Combine garlic, basil, chili, oregano, parsley, salt & pepper to make a seasoning mixture.

3. Place bread cubes into a bowl and sprinkle with the seasoning mixture. Stir a few times to coat the bread.

4. Add oil and stir.

5. Place in a non-stick frying pan or on a flat top grill. Heat over medium heat until cubes become crispy stirring often, or bake in the oven at 250° F for 15 minutes.

6. Store in a dry container out of the fridge.

7. Serve in a salad or soup.

* * *

New Brunswick has over 45 golf courses in the province. They offer from 9 to 27 holes. Some offer awe-inspiring views of rivers, lakes and the Bays of Fundy and Chaleur. Don't miss the course in St. Andrews for a stunning view of the Bay of Fundy.

Greek Style Salad

While small in number, New Brunswick's Greek community has had a strong presence in the restaurant scene. A Greek salad is always welcome on any table.

4 cups	greens of choice
1 pint	cherry tomatoes halved
1 cup	mushrooms sliced
1/2 cup	black olives sliced
1/2 cup	crushed walnuts
1/2 cup	feta cheese crumbled
1 cup	cucumber, peeled & sliced

1. Toss well and serve with a vinegar dressing on page 17.

Pita Chips

5	pita breads
1/2 cup	oil or salad dressing (eg. Italian)

1. Brush both sides of pita bread with dressing lightly.

2. Cut into bite size pieces. Place on an ungreased cookie sheet. Bake at 350° F for 10 minutes, until crispy.

3. Store in a dry airtight container, to re-crisp just re-heat.

Acadian Creamy Fiddlehead Soup

1-1/4 lb.	fiddleheads cleaned well
4 cups	stock
1 cup	evaporated milk
1 tbsp.	garlic minced
1/2 tsp.	oregano
1/2 tsp.	basil
1/2 cup	celery minced
1 tsp.	parsley
1 cup	apple sauce
1-1/2 cups	green tomatoes, chopped
Salt & pepper to taste.	

1. Purée all but 1/4 cup of fiddleheads.

2. Chop the remaining 1/4 cup of fiddleheads into small pieces, set aside.

3. Place all the ingredients in a large pot except for the milk. Simmer until the larger pieces of fiddleheads are tender. About 40 minutes on low heat.

4. Add milk and simmer 20 more minutes.

5. Serve piping hot with biscuits, bread, or dumplings.

* * *

Fiddleheads on the grocery shelf are a sure sign of spring in New Brunswick. They grow along the river banks in marshy areas. Be sure to wash them well before using.

Cream of Leek & Potato Soup

Look for farm fresh leeks and potatoes at one of New Brunswick's many Farmers Markets. With luck you will be able to pick up some delicious home made biscuits to finish off your meal.

5 cups	leeks cleaned & sliced
1/2 cup	onion diced
2 tbsp.	garlic minced
1/2 cup	mushroom minced
1 tsp.	mint
1 tsp.	rosemary
1/2 tsp.	dill
1 tsp.	green peppercorns whole
1 cup	white wine
dash	nutmeg
1 cup	evaporated milk
2 tbsp.	clarified butter
2 cups	whipping cream
4 cups	chicken or vegetable stock
3 cups	potatoes cubed

Salt & pepper to taste.

1. Place leeks, onion, garlic, and mushrooms, in a frying pan with 2 tbsps. of butter and sauté till golden brown.

2. Place sautéed mixture in a large pot, adding the mint, rosemary, dill, peppercorns, white wine, nutmeg, stock, and potatoes.

3. Simmer approximately 1 hour, stirring often. Cook until potatoes start to fall apart and crumble.

4. Whisk soup so all potatoes are dissolved, and then add cream and milk. Simmer 20 minutes on low till hot and serve.

Gifts From the Earth

Potato Skins

These make a delicious appetizer, side dish or a light lunch. Serve 1 to 2 skins per person.

1. Bake potatoes and let cool.

2. Slice potatoes in half lengthwise and scoop out the potato leaving a 1/4 inch in the shell. Retain the potato in a separate bowl.

3. Deep fry the skins till crispy, drain the grease and set aside. To reduce the fat intake you can bake skins at 400° F until crispy. They do not get as crispy and you must watch them closely.

4. Mash the potatoes adding a bit of milk. Mix in your favorite ingredients, such as broccoli, bacon bits, seafood, etc.

5. Stuff the skins with the potato mixture, (you can place 1 tsp. of sour cream in each skin before stuffing.

6. Top with shredded cheese and broil in the oven until bubbly.

* * *

Florenceville is the home of the internationally known company McCains. McCains is the world's largest processor of french fries with operations in over 40 countries.

Potato Croquettes

3 cups	potatoes, cooked, cooled & mashed
2 tbsp.	celery powder or puréed celery
2-1/2 cups	whipping cream
4 cups	fine dry bread crumbs
2 tsp.	garlic powder
2 tbsp.	onion powder
1 tsp.	cayenne pepper
2 tbsp.	dried parsley finely minced
6 eggs	well beaten
Salt & pepper to taste.	

1. For the mashed potato mixture: mix potatoes with 1 tbsp. of celery, 1 tsp. garlic, 1 tbsp. onion powder, 1/2 tsp. cayenne, 1 tbsp. parsley, 1/2 cup whipping cream, salt & pepper to taste. Mix well so all flavorings are evenly distributed.

2. Chill potato mixture for 1 hour.

3. Form potato mixture into balls or whatever shape you like. Re-chill for 1 hour.

4. Mix 4 cups bread crumbs with 1 tbsp. celery, 1 tsp. garlic powder, 1 tbsp. onion powder, 1/2 tsp. cayenne , 1 tbsp. parsley.

5. Make an egg wash consisting of 6 eggs and 2 cups of whipping cream that has been well mixed.

6. Dip balls in egg wash mixture and roll in bread crumbs until well coated.

7. Bake at 375° F for 30 minutes until crispy on a cookie sheet lightly greased.

Canadian Cheddar Cheese Sauce

Serve this sauce over steamed fresh vegetables or with a fish or chicken dish.

2 tbsp.	butter
2 tbsp.	flour
1/2 tsp.	mustard
1 cup	milk
1-1/2 cups	cheddar cheese shredded
Salt & pepper to taste.	

* Optional flavors to add to finished sauce: worcestershire sauce, soya sauce, fresh herbs, hot peppers or salsa.

1. Melt butter with mustard on low heat until evenly mixed.

2. Add flour, the mixture will be lumpy and dry, stir until all flour is absorbed.

3. Slowly add milk, stirring constantly until all of the flour mixture dissolves and the sauce is smooth.

4. Increase the heat to high, while stirring constantly until the sauce begins to thicken.

5. When the desired thickness is achieved, turn off the heat and quickly stir in the cheese. Stir until the cheese is completely melted. Serve immediately.

Hint: This sauce can be made ahead but it will be a little thinner when reheated.

Summer Lemon-Dill Rice

1-1/2 cups	water, chicken or vegetable stock
1/2 cup	lemon juice
1 tbsp.	garlic minced
1 tbsp.	dill chopped & rubbed
1/2 tsp.	salt
1 cup	rice, raw long grain
Pepper to taste.	

1. Place all ingredients except rice in a pot that has a tight fitting lid.

2. Bring to a boil.

3. Add rice, and stir well. Reduce heat to minimum and cover.

5. Cook for 20 – 30 minutes until rice is tender and fluffy.

Hint: Add some wild rice for a colorful variation.

Perfect Tempura

1 large	egg yolk
1-1/2 cups	cold water
1 cup	flour

1. Add the egg to the water and stir.

2. Add flour and stir quickly. The batter will be lumpy. Set it aside.

3. Prepare vegetables, seafood, or thin meat slices to be coated by rinsing in cold water. Pat dry. Dust food in flour to allow the batter to cling better. Set aside.

4. Dip into the batter. Deep fry or pan fry until golden.

Filo Wrapped Garden Asparagus

This easy to prepare dish is an elegant appetizer or side dish when entertaining.

2 sheets	filo pastry
4 stems	asparagus
1 tbsp.	feta cheese
1 sprig	anise (or other favorite herb)
3 tbsps.	melted butter or margarine
Salt & pepper to taste.	

1. Lay sheets of filo pastry flat on top of each other. Brush the top sheet with melted butter.

2. Layer the 4 stems of asparagus, on the top of the Filo sheets, starting at the end of the shortest side of the sheets. Layer so 2 heads of asparagus face the left and 2 face the right side.

3. Sprinkle with the Feta cheese.

4. Add salt & pepper to taste and the sprig of anise.

5. Roll the sheets up , tube-like with the asparagus inside, but roll loosely. Once rolled brush whole roll with butter.

6. Place on a non greased baking sheet. Bake at 375° F for 15 – 20 minutes until pastry is golden brown in color.

Yield: 1 appetizer.

French Scalloped Potatoes

New Brunswickers love to gather together for an evening of fun and food. This dish is perfect to tote along to a potluck.

1 cup	milk
1 tbsp.	garlic minced
1/2 cup	onion minced
1 tsp.	white pepper
1/2 tsp.	oregano
4 cups	potatoes, peeled & thinly sliced
1/4 cup	parmesan cheese
1/4 cup	cheddar shredded
Salt & pepper to taste.	

1. Mix milk, garlic, onion, white pepper, and oregano in a bowl. Set aside.

2. Cook potatoes for 10 minutes to soften them but do not cook completely.

3. Drain potatoes and place them in a deep baking dish and pour milk mixture over top.

4. Bake at 350° F for 45 minutes or until potatoes are at the desired tenderness.

5. Drain the liquid off into a small pot and bring to a slow boil being careful not to scorch the milk. Add parmesan and cheddar cheese. Stir till thickened and remove from heat.

6. Pour over potatoes and stir through gently. Broil in the oven until golden brown and serve.

Three Cheese Potatoes

Potatoes are a staple in New Brunswick kitchens. Not only do we love to grow them, we love to eat them too!

5 lbs.	potatoes, cleaned & cooked
1/2 cup	parmesan cheese powder or freshly grated
1 block	cream cheese (flavored or plain)
1/2 cup	sour cream
2 tbsp.	butter
Salt & pepper to taste.	

1. In a large bowl mash potatoes.

2. Add cheeses, sour cream, and butter.

3. Whip potatoes with a mixer.

4. Place potato mixture in a shallow baking dish so that a large surface area is exposed.

5. Bake for 15 minutes under the broiler to crisp and brown the top.

Hint: Try sprinkling shredded cheese (any flavor) over top before broiling.

Stuffed Sweet Peppers

1 cup	rice cooked
1 tsp.	garlic minced
1 tbsp.	chili powder
1 tsp.	soya sauce
1/2 cup	feta cheese
1/2 cup	fine bread crumbs
1 cup	chicken, cooked & diced
2 cups	tomato sauce
1 tsp.	basil
1 tbsp.	butter melted
1 tbsp.	worcestershire sauce
6	sweet peppers (any color)
1 cup	cheese grated

Salt & pepper to taste.

1. Cut peppers in the middle to make 2 round halves. Clean peppers out and place in a shallow baking dish. Set aside.

2. Combine rice, garlic, chili powder, soya sauce, feta cheese, bread crumbs, meat, tomato sauce, basil , 1 cup of tomato sauce, butter, worcestershire sauce and salt & pepper all together in a bowl. Mix evenly.

3. Stuff each pepper loosely. Place 1 cup of tomato sauce in bottom of pan.

4. Bake at 350° F for 25 minutes. Serve.

Hint: When cooked remove from oven. Cover with grated cheese and put under broiler till cheese is melted. You can use any cheese, parmesan, mozzarella, swiss, etc. You can use tuna, salmon, white fish, shrimp, scallops, beef, or vegetable medley.

Spicy Vegetable Stir-fry

1 cup	whole roasted almonds
4	chicken breasts sliced thinly
1 cup	green pepper sliced
1 cup	red peppers sliced
1 cup	mushrooms sliced
1 cup	onions sliced
1 cup	celery sliced
1 cup	snow peas cleaned
2 tbsps.	sesame seeds raw
1 tsp.	oil
1 tsp.	butter
1/4 tsp.	cayenne pepper
1 tsp.	chili pepper
1 tsp.	soya sauce
1 tsp.	lemon juice

1. Cook vegetables from the hardest (like the onions to softest like mushrooms adding a new one every 2 minutes) in the oil and stir often until tender.

2. Cover and let simmer for a few minutes and then add almonds, sesame seeds, and all the rest of the ingredients.

3. Cover and let cook for a few minutes.

Hint: Thicken any juice if desired with a little cornstarch mixture.

(2 tbsps. cornstarch with 1 tbsp. water).

* * *

Autumn in New Brunswick is a glorious time. The leaves are spectacular and roadside stands offer leaf lookers a chance to pick up some of the bountiful harvest.

Sautéed Garden Vegetables

If you julienne vegetables you can create a lovely decorative side dish. Always cook the hardest vegetable to the softest.

You can either pan fry or place all in a tinfoil envelope for the barbecue or oven.

1. Sauté in clarified butter with a little salt, some parsley and/or paprika, pepper, or a combination of either for 1 minute.

2. Add vegetables and cook till they are almost tender.

3. For barbecue or oven method, lay out a sheet of tinfoil and spread 2 tbsps. of butter over it. Layer on the vegetables from hardest on the bottom to softest on the top. Wrap and bake or barbecue for approximately 20-30 minutes until tender.

For vegetable suggestions try, zucchini, carrots, leeks, potatoes, sweet potatoes, squash, peppers, green tomatoes (in wedge form), celery, cabbage, or whatever else you may like.

* * *

The New Brunswick Museum in Saint John celebrates the storied past of our province. Shipbuilding, marine life, the forests and much more of our heritage is waiting to be discovered.

Steamed Asparagus or Fiddleheads

1 pound	asparagus or
1 pound	fiddleheads
1 recipe	basic béchamel sauce on page 75.

1. Clean vegetables well.

2. Steam until three quarters cooked.

3. Lay in a shallow baking dish.

4. Cover with a sauce, and bake for 15 minutes uncovered at 400° F.

5. Suggestions for sauce: dill, curry, cranberry, mustard, hot peppercorn, parmesan, cheddar, etc.

* * *

New Brunswicks' first people included the Mi'kmaqs and Maliseets. The British, French, Irish, Danes and Germans learned about the gifts of New Brunswick soil has to offer from the native people. No doubt the first taste of greens after a long hard winter. New Brunswickers still savour the first serving of fiddleheads each spring.

Spicy Chicken Wings

1/2 lb.	chicken wings per person

Sauce mixture

1/2 cup	white sugar
1/2 cup	juice from hot banana pepper rings or pickled Jalapeno
1 tsp.	garlic powder
1 tsp.	Hungarian paprika
1 tbsp.	Soya sauce

1. Mix all of the ingredients for the sauce in a deep bowl and stir until even.

2. Cut tips off chicken wings and discard, separate the wing part from the drumstick part. Quickly boil the chicken until they change color from pink to white, drain off water.

3. Coat wings with sauce and cook. Either by deep frying first, then baking them for 10 minutes with the sauce, or just bake them in the sauce for 30 minutes at 375° F.

Spicy Tacos

4 large	pita pockets
1 lb.	meat, steak, chicken, or pork
5	jalapeno peppers sliced
1 cup	onions, thinly sliced
1 cup	stock

1. Pull pita pockets apart so you have two rounds instead of 1 thick one.

2. Place meat with sliced peppers in 1 cup of stock and simmer for 15 minutes over low heat.

3. Remove meat and peppers from stock and place into a frying pan. Add onions, and 1/4 cup of stock. Fry until all liquid has evaporated.

4. In another frying pan, fry pita pockets with a little garlic butter until warm and starting to crisp. Place a portion of meat mixture in each pita and roll immediately. Secure with a tooth pick, as the pita cools it will hold its shape.

Chinese Beef

1 lb.	beef
5 tbsp.	soya sauce
1 tbsp.	flour
3 tsp.	oil
1 tsp.	white pepper
2 tsp.	cornstarch
1 lb.	bean sprouts, fresh or canned
1 tbsp.	dry sherry
1 cup	onions diced
1 tbsp.	garlic minced
4 tsp.	sugar

1. Cut meat into thin strips. Mix with 2 tbsp. of the soya sauce, and sherry, marinate for 30 minutes in the refrigerator.

2. Reserve any liquid produced.

3. Remove meat and roll in the flour until coated.

4. Heat oil in a frying pan and fry the meat and the onions for a few minutes until the meat is browned.

5. Add the marinade, to it along with the rest of soya sauce, garlic, pepper, sugar, and sprouts.

6. Simmer on low for 10 minutes, thicken any juice.

Pepper Steak Oriental

1-1/2 lbs.	beef
3 tbsp.	soya sauce
1 tsp.	oil
1/2 tsp.	ginger root or ground ginger
1 tsp.	garlic minced
6	green onions
1/2 cup	green pepper diced
2 cups	mushroom sliced
1/2 cup	beef broth
3/4 cup	firm tomatoes diced (green or red)
Salt & pepper to taste.	

1. Cut meat into strips and place into a deep bowl. Set aside.

2. In a bowl combine soya sauce, oil and salt and pepper, stir well.

3. Toss mixture over beef strips and let sit 1 hour in the refrigerator.

4. In frying pan place 1/2 tsp. oil, add ginger and garlic fry for a minute and then add beef and fry until browned.

5. Then remove meat and set it aside.

6. Add onions, peppers, and mushrooms, cook until tender, add beef and continue cooking for a few minutes.

7. Add beef stock. Simmer for 5 minutes.

8. Thicken the sauce, if desired (see method on page 24.)

Add tomatoes and toss lightly. Simmer 5 minutes on low.

Chicken Ball Sauce

1/4 cup	vinegar
1 cup	water
1/4 cup	ketchup
1/4 cup	brown sugar
1/2 cup	pineapple juice
1 tbsp.	soya sauce

1. Place all into a medium, thick based pot. Stir well. Simmer for 10 minutes over medium heat.

2. Use a cornstarch based thickener to achieve desired thickness.

Variation: Try using orange, apple, or cranberry juice in place of the pineapple juice.

Chicken Balls

1 lb.	chicken cooked, 2" squares
2 cups	pancake batter already made using 1/4 cup less liquid than called for
1 tbsp.	parsley
1 tsp.	garlic powder
3 tbsp.	soya sauce
2 tsp.	chicken stock powder
1 tbsp.	worcestershire sauce
Salt & pepper to taste.	

1. Mix all of the above ingredients well except for the chicken.

2. Dip chicken pieces into batter and fry in deep-fryer or non stick pan until crispy.

Pizza on Pita

1. Use whole wheat or plain pita bread, butter both sides with garlic butter. Then add a layer of pizza sauce.

Then layer on ingredients of choice:

onion

green pepper

tomatoes

cooked sausages

cooked hamburger

mushroom

spinach

ham

anchovies

salami

pepperoni

bacon

pineapple

hot pepper rings

etc

2. Cover with cheese, feta , mozzarella, cheddar or swiss. Cook at 350° F for 20 minutes.

Chop-Suey

1 cup	carrot sliced thin diagonally
1 cup	onion sliced thin
1 cup	green pepper sliced thin strips
1 cup	red pepper sliced thin slips
1 cup	celery sliced diagonally
1 cup	mushroom sliced thin
1/2 cup	almonds or cashews
1 tsp.	garlic minced
1 tsp.	oil
2 cups	bean sprouts , drained and rinsed
2 tbsps.	soya sauce
1/2 cup	cream of chicken soup

1. In a large frying pan or wok sauté all these vegetables from the hardest to the softest until tender.

2. Then add bean sprouts and Soya sauce. Cook all well and add cream of chicken soup, stir well.

3. Thicken if needed and serve.

Corned Beef Cakes

1-1/2 lbs.	canned corned beef, cleaned
4 cups	potatoes, cooked & cooled
1/4 cup	onion minced
1 tbsp.	garlic minced
1 tsp.	soya sauce
1 tbsp.	celery, minced
1/2 cup	bread crumbs (fine)

1. Break beef into pieces, remove any fat. Add potatoes and mix.

2. Add rest of ingredients, and mix well until even.

3. Form into 2" patties.

4. Fry in a non-stick or cast iron frying pan until crispy.

5. Serve with gravy.

* * *

Corned beef was a staple in old New Brunswick kitchens. It was a favorite of the Irish. You can almost catch a ghostly scent of corned beef and cabbage as you walk the streets of old Saint John.

Corned Beef Pie

2 lbs.	corned beef, canned & broken into small chunks
2 cups	stock beef or chicken
1 tbsp.	soya sauce
1/2 cup	onion minced
1	thick double layer pie crust
3 cups	mashed potatoes
2 cups	vegetables, corn, peas, carrots (optional)
1/2 cup	mushrooms, sliced (optional)
1/2 cup	green peppers, diced (optional)
Pepper to taste.	

1. Remove fat from beef, break into little pieces. Place into a deep pot and simmer, with all of the remaining ingredients on low heat for 20 minutes.

2. Add pepper. Cook until mixture is as thick as oatmeal. You may add mushrooms or green peppers if desired. Set aside to cool down.

3. In large deep pie pan, place the pie crust and add in layers, the corn beef mixture, vegetables if desired, and then the mashed potatoes.

4. Bake at 350° F for 30-50 minutes until crust is golden and juices are bubbly.

* * *

Remember to hide the salt shaker when you serve this meal. The settlers in New Brunswick relied on salt to cure meat and fish in order to preserve it.

Acadian Creamy Chicken Stew

Part1

4 large	chicken breasts boneless, skinless, diced
1/2 tsp.	dried dill
1 tbsp.	garlic minced
1/2 tsp.	salt
1 tbsp.	soya sauce
4 cups	chicken stock
1 tsp.	white pepper
1 cup	firm green tomato diced
1/2 cup	celery diced
1/2 cup	onion diced
1 cup	mushrooms sliced
1/2 cup	green pepper diced
1 tsp.	dried basil
1/2 cup	tomato paste
1 cup	diced carrots
1/2 cup	green peas frozen

Part 2

1 cup	diced potatoes
1 cup	cream of chicken soup
1/2 cup	sour cream

1. In a large bowl combine all of the the Part one list and simmer 10 minutes over low heat covered.

2. Add potatoes and cook on low for 20–30 minutes until potatoes are tender.

3. Add cream of chicken soup and sour cream stir well, let cook 5 more minutes and serve. Serve with a nice bread or dumplings for dipping.

Hint: For a fat reduced method use calorie reduced cream of chicken soup and light or fat free sour cream.

Chicken Donair for 1

1/2 cup	chicken, boneless, skinless, uncooked
1/2 cup	mushrooms sliced
1/4 cup	onion sliced
1/4 cup	green pepper sliced
1/2 tsp.	oil
1 tbsp.	almonds sliced optional
Salt & pepper to taste.	

1. Slice chicken thinly and fry for 1 minute in 1/2 tsp. of oil.

2. Add all the vegetables and cover with a lid. Let fry for 2 - 3 minutes. Keep stirring until chicken is cooked about 4 minutes.

3. Serve on a warmed or fried pita or tortilla shell with , donair, greek, tatziki, or ranch sauce.

Classic Garlic Bread

1 cup	butter or margarine
1 tbsp.	garlic minced
2 tbsp.	parsley
1/2 tsp.	paprika
1 loaf	bread of choice
1 cup	shredded cheese of choice

1. Cut bread in 1" thick slices, lay slices on a cookie sheet and broil in oven until lightly browned on one side only.

2. Remove from oven and let cool. Meanwhile make a garlic butter by mixing the first four ingredients until smooth.

3. Spread the butter mixture on the uncooked side of the bread and return to oven. Broil until golden brown. Sprinkle with shredded cheese and return to oven on broil until cheese is melted.

Beef Stroganoff

2 lbs.	steak or hamburger (lean)
1 cup	beef stock
1 tbsp.	soya sauce
1 cup	onions sliced thin
2 cups	mushrooms sliced
1 tbsp.	garlic minced
1/4 tsp.	mint
1/2 tsp.	pepper
1 tbsp.	worcestershire sauce
1 cup	green tomato diced
1/4 tsp.	dried basil
1 cup	sour cream
1 cup	shredded mozzarella cheese
1/4 cup	dry red wine or sherry (optional)

1. Simmer all of the above ingredients for 45 minutes on low heat stirring occasionally.

2. Add the green tomatoes and Basil.

3. Bring to a boil to reduce the liquid to half.

4. Add sour cream and mozzarella. Stir well and cook 5 more minutes on low heat. Serve.

Hint: Serve over pastry, rice, noodles, potatoes, or in a bowl with some bread for dipping.

Lasagna in a Skillet

1 envelope	dry powdered onion soup mix
1 lb.	hamburger lean
1 tsp.	oregano
3-1/2 cups	stewed tomatoes chopped fine
2 cups	stock
2 cups	half cooked noodles of choice
1/2 cup	grated parmesan cheese
1/2 cup	mozzarella cheese grated
1 tbsp.	soya sauce
1 tbsp.	dried basil
1 tbsp.	worcestershire sauce
Salt & pepper to taste.	

1. In a deep large skillet , cook beef and drain off any fat.

2. Add all of the rest of ingredients except for cheeses.

3. Stir well and bring to boil, reduce heat.

4. Stir in parmesan cheese and simmer 20 minutes, covered.

5. Sprinkle mozzarella over top and recover. Cook 5 more minutes until cheese is melted and serve.

Hint: Goes well with garlic bread and a side salad.

Grandma's Chicken Pot Pie

2 cups	chicken diced
1 cup	onion diced
2 cups	carrots diced
1 cup	mushroom sliced
1 cup	frozen green peas
1 tbsp.	garlic minced
1 tbsp.	soya sauce
2 cups	cream of chicken soup
1 cup	cream of mushroom soup
1 cup	evaporated can milk
1/2 cup	sour cream
1 cup	chicken broth
1/2 cup	red pepper diced
1	pie crust

Salt and pepper to taste.

1. Place in a large pot, chicken and broth, bring to a slow boil until chicken is cooked.

2. Add all vegetables and cook until almost tender.

3. Add everything else and simmer one half hour on low heat.

4. Place mixture in a large deep baking dish, leaving enough room for a pie crust.

5. Loosely crumble pie crust on top of dish.

6. Bake at 350° F for 20–35 minutes until crust is flaky and golden brown.

*Instead of pie crust you can use your favorite tea biscuit or dumpling recipe.

Chicken à la King Casserole

2 cups	chicken, boneless, skinless & diced
1 tsp.	soya sauce
1 tsp.	garlic minced
dash	olive oil or clarified butter
1 cup	frozen green peas
1 cup	red pepper minced
1 cup	onion minced
1 cup	mushrooms sliced
1 cup	cream of mushroom soup
1 cup	cream of chicken soup
1/2 cup	sour cream
Salt & pepper to taste.	

1. In large pot fry the chicken until browned.

2. Reduce heat to a medium temperature, add onion, stirring often until onion starts to turn clear. Then add the rest of the vegetables and spices, stirring well to distribute evenly.

3. Add cream of mushroom soup and cream of chicken soup and stir well. Then add 1/2 cup of sour cream.

4. Stir well and let simmer on low heat for 20 minutes. Serve piping hot, as a stew, over rice, toast, pan-fries, or in a tart shell.

Smoked hot green chili peppers or 2 cups of crushed stewed tomatoes and 1 tbsp. of dried basil, add a zing to the dish.

Good Morning Omelette

6	eggs
4 tbsp.	cold water
1/4 cup	red pepper diced
1/4 tsp.	garlic minced
1/4 cup	onion diced
1/4 cup	green pepper diced
1/4 cup	firm green tomato diced
1/2 cup	cooked ham * optional
1 tsp.	clarified butter
Salt & pepper to taste.	

1. Beat eggs and 2 tbsps. of the cold water until frothy about 2 minutes.

2. Place all other ingredients into a hot frying pan, and sauté until almost cooked.

3. Add egg mixture and stir constantly until all vegetables are distributed evenly into the egg and then cover immediately, reducing heat to low.

4. Wait 1 minute then add 1 tsp. of cold water down the inside edge of pan and cover again. The steam that is produced will cook the top of the egg.

5. When top of egg is cooked, turn off heat, spread shredded cheese over half of the surface of the egg and fold over the other half on top of the cheese.

6. Add 1 tsp. of cold water again cover and remove from heat. Let stand 2 minutes.

*You can substitute bacon or sausage for the ham.

Almond & Red Pepper Stir-fry

4	chicken boneless, skinless
1 tsp.	butter
1 tbsp.	garlic minced
1 cup	almonds sliced or slivered
1 cup	onion sliced
2 cups	red pepper sliced

1. Slice chicken thinly and fry in butter until golden brown.

2. Add garlic, almonds and onions.

3. Continue to fry for 7 -10 minutes, stirring often.

4. Add red pepper and cover. Let cook 5 more minutes.

5. Serve over Summer Lemon Dill Rice page 43.

* * *

A complete Chinese meal gives everyone a reason to hang around the stove. New Brunswickers' love kitchen parties, so enlist your friends to cook up the variety of Chinese recipes in this book. See the recipes as such; Chop-Suey page 58, Pepper Steak Oriental page 55, or Chinese Beef on page 54.

Chicken Sandwich

1/2 cup	almonds sliced & roasted
3/4 cup	red pepper sliced thin
1/2 cup	onions sliced thin
**1 breast	chicken (3 oz.)
2 slices	crusty bread, lightly toasted
*2 tbsps.	cream cheese
Salt & pepper to taste.	

1. Sauté almonds, red pepper and onions in garlic butter until caramelized. Set aside.

2. Fry chicken until crispy. Slice into thin strips.

3. Using thinly sliced crusty bread, lightly toasted, layer on the following ingredients in this order: one slice of bread, cream cheese, hot chicken, vegetables, remaining cream cheese, the other slice of bread.

4. Place in the oven for 3 – 5 minutes on 350° F to bind the sandwich together. The heat will melt the cream cheese a little.

* Other cheeses may be substituted, Brie or Camembert are delicious options.

** Chicken can be pre-cooked or canned. Any meat can be substituted.

* * *

After a day on the water or a trip to the Reversing Falls, a quick and easy supper will be in order. For those brave souls who observed the falls first hand from a jet boat, ask someone else to man the stove. You deserve it!

Golden Honey Garlic Sauce

1 cup	honey
2 cups	water
2 tbsp.	garlic minced
1/4 cup	soya sauce
1 tbsp.	butter
1/2 tsp.	salt
1/2 tsp.	white pepper

1. Place all of the above ingredients in a pot and stir until well mixed.

2. Bring mixture to a slow boil over medium heat. Remove from heat.

3. Thicken with cornstarch method if desired, or pour over meat and bake. (eg. ribs, chicken, pork, fish etc.).

Grilled Honey Glazed Chicken

1	golden honey garlic sauce recipe (above)
2 lbs.	chicken pieces of choice

1. Par boil chicken pieces (if they have bone), this reduces the complete cooking time, tenders the meat and removes most of the fat content.

2. Place on the grill and baste continually with the honey sauce for the rest of cooking time. You can just keep dipping whole piece in sauce and return to grill.

Creamy Tarragon & Mushroom Sauce

A lovely sauce for pork and chicken or try it over fresh steamed vegetables.

2 tbsp.	butter or margarine
1 cup	mushrooms sliced
1/4 cup	white wine
1 tbsp.	brandy or liquor of choice
1-1/4 cup	whipping cream
1 tsp.	cornstarch
2 tsp.	cold water
1 tbsp.	green onion or fresh chives chopped
1 tsp.	dried tarragon*
1 tbsp.	worcestershire sauce
Salt & pepper to taste.	

1. Melt butter in a skillet and sauté mushrooms till tender.

2. Add the wine and brandy and simmer for 5 minutes on low.

3. Mix cornstarch and water. Gradually add to skillet, stirring constantly. Simmer for 3 minutes.

4. Remove from heat and add cream, tarragon, onion, chives, salt and pepper. Stir well. Return to stove to heat just before using.

* Try other herbs such as mint, basil, cayenne, for different flavors.

Creamy Alfredo Sauce

1 cup	milk
1 cup	whipping cream
1/2 cup	parmesan cheese grated
1 tbsp.	garlic butter
1 tsp.	parsley
Salt & pepper to taste.	

1. Bring all of the ingredients to a boil on medium to high heat without burning the milk. Stir constantly.

2. As the liquid is boiling, add 1/2 cup parmesan cheese and continue to stir constantly. Cheese will thicken the sauce instantly. Remove from heat and use immediately as a sauce or a base for a casserole.

Spicy Tomato Sauce

4 cups	stewed tomatoes, chopped fine
1/2 cup	onion minced
1 tbsp.	garlic minced
1 tsp.	cayenne pepper
1 tbsp.	chili powder
1/4 cup	crushed chilies
1/2 cup	Tabasco sauce
1 tsp.	basil dried
1 tbsp.	parsley
Salt & pepper to taste.	

1. Blend all ingredients in a large deep bowl until evenly mixed.

2. Let sit at room temperature for 1 hour before using, so the flavors can blend.

Hint: Use as a relish, a salsa or as a cooking sauce. Serve hot or cold.

White Sauce aka Béchamel Sauce

3 tbsps.	butter
6 tbsps.	flour
1 cup	whole milk
Salt & pepper to taste.	

1. Melt butter over low heat in a thick based sauce pan. Slowly add the flour until all is absorbed by the butter.

2. While whisking, slowly add the milk and continue to stir until all is smooth.

3. Gradually increase the heat to medium, and continue to stir until mixture begins to thicken. Keep stirring till mixture becomes as thick as corn syrup and then remove from heat.

4. Remember once you remove it is still hot and will continue to thicken on its own for a minute or so. This sauce is better used right away, when cooled and then reheated it may need to be thinned, and may not be smooth.

Hint: This sauce is good used in a variety of ways , in a dish that needs a little bit more moisture or some creaminess. In a dish that you just want a sauce but not a lot of additional flavor. In lasagna as a layer in between the noodles.

Hint: For a flavored white sauce; add any one or combination of these items as soon as you remove sauce from heat: curry 1 tsp.; parsley 1 tbsp.; mushroom 1 cup cooked, minced or sliced; cooked onion 1/2 cup minced; dill 1 tbsp. dried; mustard 2 tbsp.; 1/2 cup cranberries crushed or whole plus 1 tbsp. brown sugar.

Dough Boys or Dumplings

These bread like additions to soups and stews, served as an extra filler in the Saturday night soup pot. They can also take the place of potatoes in a stew.

2 cups	flour
1/2 tsp.	salt
2 tsp.	baking powder
1 tbsp.	white sugar
2 tbsp.	butter or margarine (soft)
1 cup	cold water

1. Sift all dry ingredients well in a large deep bowl.

2. Add butter and rub into flour mixture until all is crumbly.

3. Add enough cold water, about 1/2 to 3/4 cup, enough to stick dough together roughly so that it is a little wet but not too dry. It should be slightly tacky to your fingers.

4. Drop spoon size or larger into a liquid based dish for the final 10 – 15 minutes of cooking time.

5. Cover and let steam on the top of your dish for 10 -15 minutes.

* * *

New Brunswick is Canada's only official bilingual province. Approximately one third of its' population speak French. Acadian French is different in some ways from that spoken in Quebec and in France, reflecting their own unique heritage.

Good Old Hamburger Stew

1 lb.	extra lean hamburger
4 cups	stewed tomatoes chopped
1 cup	tomato soup
1 cup	onion chopped
2 cups	carrots chopped
1 cup	mushrooms sliced
1/2 cup	tomato paste
2 cups	potatoes diced
1 tsp.	mint
1 tbsp.	basil
1 tsp.	oregano
1 tbsp.	fresh garlic minced
1/2 cup	celery chopped
1 cup	green pepper diced
3 cups	beef stock
1 large	bay leaf
Salt & pepper to taste.	

1. Place all of the ingredients except for the potatoes, in a large stew pot. Let simmer on low heat stirring often for 1 hour.

2. Add potatoes and cook for 30 minutes more .

3. Serve piping hot.

Creamy Peppercorn Sauce

This is delicious served over steak or chicken. It also lends itself well to dishes baked in the oven or as a flavoring for gravy.

1-1/4 cup	whipping cream
2 tbsp.	green or black peppercorns
2 tbsp.	white wine
1 tsp.	chicken stock powder
1 tsp.	mustard
1 tbsp.	worcestershire sauce
2 tsp.	cornstarch
3 tbsp.	cold water
1 tbsp.	chives or green onions chopped
Salt & pepper to taste.	

1. In a pot, combine cream, peppercorns, wine, chicken stock powder, mustard and worcestershire sauce. Stir over low heat.

2. Increase heat till mixture comes to a boil and then turn down heat until the mixture is just under a boil.

3. Mix cornstarch and water and gradually stir into the cream mixture stirring constantly.

4. Remove from heat and add chives.

Tenderloin Tips

1-1/2 lbs.	top round or marinating sirloin steak
1 cup	water or stock
2 tbsp.	soya sauce
1/2 tsp.	garlic minced
1/2 tsp.	pepper
1 cup	onion sliced
1 tbsp.	worcestershire sauce
1 tbsp.	beef stock powder dissolved in water.
Few drops	gravy browning
Dash of chili pepper.	

1. Brown the meat, in a large skillet for 5 minutes and add 1 cup of onions.

2. Cook over medium heat, stirring often until the onions are golden, for about 7-10 minutes.

3. Add everything else and stir well. Cover and let simmer on low for 45 minutes stirring occasionally.

4. Remove cover and bring liquid to a boil and thicken.

5. Mushrooms or green pepper may be added.

Serve over Spiced Rice (see recipe on page 12.) or a bed of mashed potatoes.

Quiche

6	eggs
1 cup	milk
1/2 tsp.	garlic powder
2 cups	commercial tea biscuit mix

1. In a large bowl combine all ingredients.

2. Beat by hand for about 5 minutes.

3. Pour into a greased baking dish and bake 400° F for 25 to 35 minutes until fluffy and dish springs back. Do not open the oven door for the first 20 minutes as the Quiche may fall. The quiche will shrink as it cools.

Hint: You can create a flavored quiche by adding meat and/or vegetables before baking. Prepare meat and vegetables and place them in the baking dish before pouring the quiche mixture in. For ingredients try broccoli and Cheddar cheese, broccoli and Swiss cheese, ham and cheese, mushroom and mozzarella, ham and Swiss, tomatoes and cheese, tomato and sausage, tomatoes and broccoli, tomatoes and herbs, any spices and/or herbs.

Oven Swiss Steak

1-1/2 lbs.	beef (choice of cut)
1/4 cup	flour
1 tbsp.	olive oil
2 cups	stewed tomatoes, chopped or crushed
1/2 cup	celery diced
1/2 cup	onion diced
1 tsp.	worcestershire sauce
Optional	1/2 cup green pepper and mushrooms
Salt & pepper to taste.	

1. Cut meat into strips or bite size pieces.

2. Rub flour into the meat and brown the meat in a frying pan with oil. Reserve the drippings.

3. Transfer meat into a deep baking dish and add pan drippings, tomatoes, celery, onion, and Worcestershire sauce.

4. Bake 1-1/2 hours in a 350° F oven until smooth and bubbly.

5. Serve over mashed potatoes or try the Classic Three Cheese Potato recipe on page 46.

Saturday Meatloaf

2 cups	bread crumbs
1 cup	cream of mushroom soup
3 lbs.	lean ground beef
2 eggs	beaten
1 cup	onion minced
1 tsp.	garlic minced
1/4 tsp.	mint

Sauce:

1 cup	ketchup
1 cup	brown sugar
2 tbsp.	mustard
Salt & pepper to taste.	

1. In a large deep bowl combine the bread crumbs, cream of mushroom soup, eggs, salt & pepper, onion, garlic, and mint until all the breadcrumbs are wet.

2. Add meat and mix evenly.

3. Place into a loaf pan or pan of choice and bake at 350° F for 1 hour. Drain grease.

4. Mix sauce using ketchup, brown sugar, and mustard. Pour over meatloaf and return to oven for 20 minutes.

* For easier serving portions and shorter cooking time use a muffin pan for baking individual loaves.

Chicken & Garden Broccoli Stir-fry

4	chicken breasts, boneless, skinless
1 head	broccoli, florets only
1 cup	slivered almonds
1 tbsp.	garlic minced
1/4 tsp.	dried dill (very important)
1/2 cup	onion sliced
1/2 cup	chicken broth
1 tsp.	olive oil
Salt & pepper to taste.	

1. Cut chicken into thin strips and fry in hot pan with olive oil till slightly browned.

2. Add the garlic, dill and salt & pepper. Fry just another minute.

3. Add the almonds, onions and broth .

4. Let simmer for 10 minutes until onions just start to become transparent.

5. Add the broccoli florets, stir and let simmer. Cover for 5 minutes. Take off the cover and thicken the liquid.

6. Serve over a bed of rice.

Meatballs

5 lbs.	lean hamburger
3 cups	bread crumbs
1/4 cup	garlic minced
1 tsp.	chili powder
2 eggs	beaten
2 tbsp.	cold water
1/2 cup	oatmeal
1 cup	milk
2 cups	ketchup
1 cup	molasses
3 cups	brown sugar
1/2 cup	mustard
1 cup	diced onions
4 – 8 cups	beef broth

Salt & pepper to taste.

1. Place bread crumbs, garlic, chili powder, eggs, cold water, oatmeal, milk, onions, salt & pepper into a large deep bowl and mix thoroughly. Add meat and remix.

2. Roll into 1 oz balls. Use an ice cream scoop or shot glass to measure. Roll into tight uniform balls. Bake at 350° F in oven for 1 hour. Drain pan, pour off grease and retain the juice.

3. In a large pot combine drippings from meatballs, ketchup, brown sugar, molasses, mustard. Mix until even. Add meatballs. Fill the pot with beef stock until the meatballs are covered by liquid (approx. 4 – 8 cups). Stir well so all is mixed evenly. Simmer on low for 1 hour. The sauce will reduce and coat the meatballs. Remove the meatballs and simmer sauce for 30 minutes until it reduces and thickens. Place meatballs back in the sauce to heat for about 10 minutes and serve.

Lemon Orange Chicken

1 cup	lemon juice
1 cup	orange juice
1 tsp.	dill
1 tbsp.	parsley
1 cup	chicken stock
1 tbsp.	garlic butter
2 lbs.	chicken or pieces
Salt & pepper to taste.	

1. Season meat with salt and pepper and set aside.

2. Boil lemon juice, orange juice, dill, parsley, chicken stock, garlic butter until bubbly and then reduce heat a little so it is still at a low boil. Let sauce reduce one third.

3. Place cleaned chicken in a shallow baking dish and pour the sauce over top.

4. Bake at 350° F for 1-1/2 hours. Stirring occasionally.

5. Garnish with slices of lemon and orange.

* * *

In the early 1800's King's Square was part of the outskirts of the city of Saint John. It served as both a market and a dump. In 1848 the walkways were laid in the pattern of the British flag, the Union Jack. Many of the older trees that shade the park benches were planted during Centennial celebrations in 1883.

Lemon Lime Mustard Bake

4	chicken pieces, boneless, skinless
1 cup	mustard
1/2 cup	lime juice
1/2 cup	lemon juice
1 tsp.	garlic minced
1/2 cup	chives or green onions chopped
1 tbsp.	white sugar
Salt & pepper to taste.	

1. Combine mustard, lime juice, lemon juice, garlic, chives, salt & pepper, and sugar in a bowl until evenly mixed.

2. Place chicken breasts in a shallow baking dish spaced evenly apart.

3. Pour sauce over the chicken breasts. Cover.

4. Bake at 350° F for 1-1/2 hours. Check twice during the cooking process. Serve.

Chicken Cordon Blue

This recipe takes a bit of time to prepare. It will be easiest if all ingredients are organized before beginning.

4	slices of mozzarella or Swiss cheese
4	thin slices of cooked ham or Prosciutto
4 tsps.	jam (strawberry or raspberry)
1/2 cup	onion minced
1/2 cup	red peppers diced
1 cup	mushrooms sliced
1 cup	slivered almonds
1 tbsp.	garlic minced
1 cup	cream of chicken soup
1 cup	cream of mushroom soup
2	eggs
1/4 cup	milk
1 cup	cornstarch
4	chicken breasts, boneless, skinless
1/4 cup	olive oil
Salt & pepper to taste.	

1. Pound chicken pieces flat with a meat mallet. Lie flat and season with salt and pepper. Set aside.

2. Layer 1 slice of mozzarella cheese, 1 slice of meat, 1 tsp. of jam spread evenly on top of each piece of chicken. Roll up fairly tight and set aside.

3. Make an egg wash with 2 eggs and 1/4 cup of milk beaten together. Dip chicken pieces in wash and then roll in cornstarch to coat, set aside.

4. Fry in a hot pan until all sides are browned. Set aside.

5. In a frying pan sauté, garlic, onions, almonds, and red pepper until onions are just slightly transparent.

6. Reduce the heat to low and add chicken and soups. Mix evenly.

7. In a deep baking dish, place chicken breasts spaced evenly apart. Pour the sauce mixture over top.

8. Bake at 325° F for 1-1/2 hours stirring twice during the

cooking process.

Serve piping hot, on a bed of rice or the Three Cheese Potato recipe on page 46.

* * *

A trip to the Acadian Historical Village in Caraquet will take you back in time to the 1700's. True Acadian food, songs, music and dance can be experienced first hand.

Cabbage Rolls

Meat mixture

2 cups	ground meat *
1 cup	onion minced
3/4 cup	feta cheese
1/4 cup	parmesan cheese
1/2 cup	fine bread crumbs
1 tbsp.	garlic minced
1/4 tsp.	dried basil
Salt & pepper to taste.	

Sauce

3 cups	crushed tomatoes
1 cup	firm plum tomatoes, chopped
1 cup	tomato sauce
1 cup	tomato paste
2 cups	tomato juice
1 cup	tomato soup
1 tbsp.	dried basil
1 tsp.	garlic minced
1 tsp.	oregano
2 tbsp.	soya sauce
2 tbsp.	worcestershire sauce
Salt & pepper to taste.	

1. You first have to cook the cabbage head partially to loosen the leaves. In a large pot three quarters full of water cut around stump core of cabbage with a sharp knife and place stump down into the hot water, reduce heat. As the cabbage begins to cook, slowly loosen leaves of cabbage and remove from water to cool.

Set aside.

2. Prepare a meat mixture and roll a portion inside each leaf. Place all ingredients for meat mixture into a deep large bowl and mix until even and smooth.

3. Place 1-3 tbsps. of meat mixture inside each leaf depending on the size of the leaf. Roll up firmly so the leaves will stay together but not so tight to inhibit cooking.

4. Place all rolled leaves in a deep baking dish or roaster pan spaced loosely so the air can circulate around them.

5. To make the sauce, combine all ingredients in the list in a deep mixing bowl. Stir until smooth. Pour sauce over rolls and bake for 2 hours at 325° F. Stir every 30 minutes.

Serve over rice.

Hint: for a spicier flare add your favorite hot sauce or spicy herb to the meat or sauce mixture.

Hint: This dish can be made with any type of meat, chicken, fish, pork, beef, or even vegetarian with a tofu or bean replacement.

* You can use raw meat but you will be unable to drain any grease.

Italian Pasta with Cheese

4 cups	spaghetti sauce
2 lbs.	lean hamburger meat
1 cup	sour cream
1 cup	cream of chicken soup
2 cups	mushrooms sliced
2 cups	shredded mozzarella
6 cups	partially cooked pasta
1 tbsp.	garlic minced
1 tbsp.	dried basil
1 tsp.	oregano
1 cup	onion minced
Salt & pepper to taste.	

1. Cook hamburger meat & mushrooms, drain grease and reserve drippings.

2. Add spaghetti sauce to meat, stir well.

3. Add sour cream, cream of chicken soup, 1 cup of mozzarella cheese, garlic, basil, oregano, and onion. Stir well.

4. Toss in the pasta and stir until pasta is well covered. Place into a large deep baking dish.

5. Bake for 45 minutes at 300° F, stirring twice during the cooking process.

6. Remove from oven, stir and then place 1 cup of shredded cheese over top and return to oven. Broil until cheese is melted and bubbly.

Honey Roasted Garlic Chicken

2 lbs.	chicken pieces
12 cloves	garlic, cleaned & sliced thin
1 cup	honey
2 tbsp.	soya sauce
1/2 cup	stock
Salt & pepper to taste.	

1. Place chicken in shallow baking dish and sprinkle with the garlic. Set aside.

2. In a saucepan quickly bring the water, honey, soya sauce, salt & pepper to a boil.

3. Mix well. Pour over the chicken and bake at 350° F for 1-1/2 hours. You may want to thicken the sauce.

HINT: If you parboil your chicken this tenderizes the meat and reduces the fat content of the meat as well. Save the liquid from the parboil and use in place of the stock.

Treasures From the Sea

Treasures from the Sea

Maritime Clam Chowder

3 cups	baby clams, cleaned & uncooked (or canned clams, save the juice)
1/2 cup	onion diced
1 cup	mushroom sliced
1 tbsp.	parsley
1 tsp.	rosemary rubbed
1 tbsp.	butter
1 tsp.	chili powder
1/2 tsp.	dill dried
2 cups	potatoes diced
1/2 cup	green tomato diced
1/4 cup	bacon, crispy & finely chopped
1 cup	whipping cream
1 cup	cream of chicken soup or skim milk
2 cups	evaporated milk
5 cups	chicken or vegetable stock
Salt & pepper to taste.	

1. Place all of the ingredients into a large deep pot and simmer on low until potatoes are done. About 1 hour.

Authentic Seafood Pasta Sauce

1/2 lb.	fresh raw mussels (in the shell)
2 cups	canned baby clams with juice
1/2 lb.	fresh raw clams (in the shell)
1 cup	cleaned small shrimp
2 cups	mushroom sliced
1/2 cup	onion minced
1/2 cup	celery minced
1 cup	beef stock
2 cups	crushed tomatoes
1 cup	tomato soup
1 cup	tomato paste
1 cup	zucchini diced (not quite ripe so it is firmer)
1 tbsp.	garlic minced
1 tsp.	oregano
1 tsp.	parsley
1 tsp.	basil
1/2 tsp.	mint
Salt & pepper taste.	

1. Place all of the ingredients into a large deep pot and simmer for 2 hours on low.

2. Serve over a bed of pasta.

3. Top with grated parmesan or Romano cheese.

Goes great with any type of pasta.

Delicious Oysters Rockefeller

2 lbs.	oysters
1/4 cup	bacon, crispy & minced
2 cups	spinach, cleaned & minced
1/4 cup	onion minced
1/2 cup	very fine bread crumbs
1/4 cup	Tabasco sauce
1/2 cup	oyster juice
1/2 cup	parmesan cheese freshly grated
1 tbsp.	black licorice flavored liquor (Anisette)

1. Clean oysters, spread them onto a cookie sheet. Open them flat so they are on the half shell. Set aside.

2. In a bowl mix all of the ingredients except for the parmesan cheese until well blended. Spoon a 1–2 tbsps. portion on top of each oyster.

3. Top each oyster with parmesan cheese and broil in oven until browned.

4. Serve 6 per person as an hors-d'oeuvre or 18 as a meal.

* * *

Malpeque oysters are one of New Brunswick's famous local treasures.

Savvy Seafood Spread

1 cup	seafood of choice
1 cup	herbed or regular cream cheese softened
1 tsp.	white pepper
1 tsp.	dill dried
1/4 tsp.	garlic powder
1 tbsp.	worcestershire sauce
1/4 tsp.	paprika
1/4 tsp.	chili powder

1. Use cooked fresh seafood that has been cooled or canned. Use shrimp, salmon, or crab or combination of all three.

2. Blend all ingredients well in a food processor until even and smooth. Chill 2 hours before serving.

3. Serve with food like a sliced baguette, cucumbers, carrots, red and green pepper, celery, sliced melons, or apples, or heat the mixture in a double boiler and then serve over pasta, potatoes or even in a quiche.

Goes great as a sandwich meat, on squares of crispy bread or for dipping vegetables and crackers.

Creamy Co Co St. Jacques Scallops in the Half Shell

1 tsp.	parsley
1/4 cup	bacon, crispy & minced
1 tbsp.	lemon juice
1 tbsp.	onion minced
1/4 cup	white wine
2 lbs.	scallops
1 tbsp.	clarified butter
1 tbsp.	garlic minced
1/2 cup	whipping cream
4 cups	potatoes, cooked, & whipped
1 cup	dried parmesan cheese

Salt & pepper to taste.

1. Slice scallops into thin and tiny bite size pieces or use baby scallops cut in half.

2. Sauté the scallops, garlic and onion in butter until tender. Add parsley, bacon, lemon juice, white wine, salt & pepper, and sauté one more minute. Add cream and simmer on low heat for a few more minutes stirring constantly until the cream is absorbed.

3. Lay the shells on a cookie sheet and place a heaping spoon of the mixture in the center of each shell. Pipe a tube of creamy mashed potatoes around until you reach the outside edge of the shell.

5. Sprinkle each shell with 1 tsp. dried parmesan and broil in oven until golden.

6. Serve as an appetizer allowing 2 per person or as a main meal of 4 per person with a side of Summer Lemon Dill Rice on page 43, or Spice Rice page 12, and a side salad of greens.

Yield: 20 – 24 shells, you can use real shells cleaned, individual mini tart pans, or you can purchase these shells in a cooking store.

* Fat Free: You can use skim milk or cheese to reduce the fat. Or even use fat free cream of chicken or cream of mushroom soup in place of the cream.

* I like to add 1/2 cup whipping cream, 1 tsp. pepper, and 1/4 cup cream cheese and whip my potatoes for 4 minutes with the food processor or mixer.

Mariners' Sautéed Scallops

1 tbsp.	clarified butter
1 tsp.	garlic minced
1 tbsp.	onion minced
1 tbsp.	lemon juice
1/2 lb.	scallops

1. In a hot frying pan, heat butter, toss in scallops, garlic and onion and stir constantly over medium to high heat for 3 minutes. Reduce heat and simmer on low for 3 minutes covered.

2. Remove cover, increase heat to reduce any liquid. Add lemon juice and let reduce again.

3. Serve on a bed of Summer Lemon Dill Rice from page 43, or Spiced Rice on page 12.

4. Serves two.

* * *

Digby scallops are much larger than the lake variety. They are also more flavourful.

Hot Atlantic Shrimp Dip

This dish is great whenever a group gathers. Delicious with shrimp, it also works well with salmon, tuna, crab, scallop, lobster or chicken.

1 cup	herbed or plain cream cheese softened
2 cups	cooked or canned shrimp
1 tbsp.	green onion minced
1 tbsp.	lemon juice
1 tsp.	jalapeno pepper minced or puréed
1/4 cup	sour cream
1 tsp.	cayenne pepper
1 tsp.	garlic minced
1/2 tsp.	paprika
1 tbsp.	soya sauce
1 tbsp.	worcestershire sauce
Salt & pepper to taste.	

1. Purée all of the above ingredients in a food processor or blender until smooth.

2. Spread in a shallow casserole dish and bake for 15 minutes on 350°F until bubbly. Serve with crusty bread, nacho chips or pita chips for dipping or place in an air tight container and cool for 2 hours before using.

Serve cold, with vegetables and crackers or hot on a toasted bread.

Fisherman Style Fish Cakes

2 lbs.	fresh fish (eg. cod or Boston blue, canned shrimp, lobster, tuna or salmon).
1 tsp.	black pepper
1 tsp.	garlic minced
1/4 cup	onion minced
1/4 cup	bread crumbs
1 tbsp.	flour
4 cups	potatoes
1/2 tsp.	dried dill
Salt to taste.	

1. Cook and debone the fish, cook and mash potatoes, and let cool.

2. Mix all of the ingredients in a deep bowl until evenly blended. Shape into 2-1/2" flat circles and fry in a hot frying pan over medium heat until golden brown on each side.

Atlantic Salmon Patties

2 lbs.	salmon, cooked, cleaned & flaked
4 cups	potatoes cooked, cooled & mashed
1/4 cup	flour
1 tbsp.	onion minced
1 tbsp.	celery minced
1/2 cup	bread crumbs (fine)
1/4 cup	parmesan cheese
1/4 cup	bacon bits minced
1 tbsp.	garlic minced
1/4 cup	melted butter
Salt & pepper to taste.	

1. Combine all of the ingredients in a large bowl, mixing well.

2. Form into round thin circles about 1" thick , and fry until crisp.

Atlantic Apricot Shrimp

2 lbs.	raw shrimp cleaned
2 cups	snow peas
1 cup	dried apricots
1 cup	slivered almonds, toasted
1 tsp.	garlic minced
1 tbsp.	butter
Salt & pepper to taste.	

1. Soak apricots in hot water for 30 minutes to revitalize them. Slice thinly and retain the juice from soaking.

2. Fry the apricots over low heat for a few minutes, in butter. Add the snow peas and shrimp, salt & pepper. Fry until shrimp are pink & tender, about 8 -15 minutes, stirring often but gently. Toss in the almonds and stir well.

3. If there is any juice, thicken it with a little cornstarch, follow the recipe on page 24 for this procedure.

4. Serve over a bed of spinach pasta, cayenne pepper pasta, or Alfredo linguine.

Hint: You should serve some garlic bread with this one, the flavor mixtures of salt, sweet, garlic, crispy, and nutty are like no other.

* * *

The Bay of Fundy tides can rise up to 48 feet (14 metres). That is high enough to submerge a four storey building. They bring with them 100 billion tons of water.

Acadian Shrimp fry

1 tbsp.	olive oil
1 cup	carrots sliced
1 cup	onions sliced
1 tbsp.	garlic minced
1 cup	celery sliced
1 cup	snow peas cut in half
2 lbs.	shrimp
1 tsp.	white pepper
1 tsp.	parsley
1/2 tsp.	fresh dill minced
1/2 tsp.	rosemary rubbed
1/2 cup	green pepper sliced
1/2 cup	red pepper sliced
1/2 cup	yellow peppers sliced
1 cup	mushrooms sliced
2 tbsps.	lemon juice

1. Heat oil in a large deep frying pan until hot. Add carrots, onions, garlic, celery, snow peas and cook for 2 minutes stirring constantly.

2. Add shrimp, all the peppers and spices. Reduce heat to medium and stir every 30 seconds for 5 minutes.

3. Turn off heat. Cover and let steam for 3 minutes. Shrimp should be pink and plump and peppers just turning tender. Serve over a bed of rice or pasta with a nice side salad of greens.

Variation: You can substitute scallops for the shrimp.

Garden Broccoli wrapped with Atlantic Salmon

8 fillets	salmon
1 bunch	broccoli
2	eggs
1/4 cup	warm water
2 tbsp.	clarified butter
1/2 tsp.	salt
1 tsp.	white pepper
2 tbsp.	garlic minced
1 tsp.	cayenne pepper
1 tsp.	chili pepper

1. Cut broccoli off at the top of the stem so that the broccoli florets have stems 3 inches long. Wash, clean and set aside.

2. Clean fish and set aside.

3. Make an egg bath of eggs, warm water, butter, salt, pepper, garlic, cayenne, and chili. Beat well until evenly mixed.

4. Dip fillets in egg bath. Lay fillets flat. Place 2 broccoli florets on each fillet, parallel but with the heads at opposite ends. Roll so broccoli florets heads are coming out each side. Place on a lightly greased cookie sheet spaced evenly apart.

5. Cover with a tinfoil cap for each bundle. Bake at 400° F for 15 – 20 minutes until fish is tender.

Serve on a bed of rice.

* * *

Atlantic salmon were once plentiful in our rivers. They attracted sport fishermen from near and far. Now salmon fishing is strictly limited. Much of our salmon now comes from fish farms.

Sautéed Garlic Shrimp with Sweet Peppers

2 lbs.	raw shrimp cleaned
1 entire	bulb of garlic sliced thinly
1/2 cup	onion thinly sliced
1/2 tsp.	white pepper
1/2 tsp.	salt
1/2 tsp.	fresh dill
1 tbsp.	olive oil
1/2 tsp.	chili powder
1 cup	red pepper sliced
1 cup	yellow pepper sliced

1. In a large deep frying pan heat oil, add onions and garlic. Cook, over medium heat stirring constantly for 3 minutes.

2. Add shrimp and toss well, soon as the shrimp start to turn pink add peppers, chili powder, salt & pepper.

3. Cover and let steam over low heat for 5 minutes stirring frequently but gently. As soon as peppers start to turn tender, remove from heat.

Serve over the Summer Lemon Dill Rice recipe on page 43, or try it with the Three Cheese Potatoes on page 46, for a delicious combination.

Spicy Fundy Fish Fillets

3 lbs.	fish fillets *
2	egg whites beaten
1 tsp.	chili powder
1 tsp.	garlic powder
2 tsp.	cayenne powder
1 tsp.	onion powder
1/4 cup	warm water
Salt & pepper to taste.	

1. Make egg wash with egg whites, chili, garlic, cayenne, onion powder, salt & pepper and water. Mix well.

2. Dip each piece of fish into the egg wash. Fry each piece separately in a fairly hot pan. Cover the pan with a tight fitted lid as this will form a hotter heat seal to make the fish crispy.

3. Fry for 2 – 5 minutes per side depending on thickness of fillet. Keep cooked pieces warm in the oven on low temperature.

* White fish like cod, Boston blue or haddock go well in this recipe. Salmon may be used but needs careful handling as it is a delicate fish once cooked.

* * *

The Bay of Fundy is known for its seals, porpoises, seabirds, and 15 different types of whales. One of the world's rarest is the Right Whale. There are estimated to be less than 350 left.

Pacific Deep Dish Salmon Pie

2	deep dish 9" pie crust
2 lbs.	salmon cooked & cleaned
1/4 cup	onion minced
1/4 cup	celery minced
1/2 cup	red pepper minced
1 tsp.	garlic minced
1 tsp.	white pepper
1/2 tsp.	salt
1 tbsp.	lemon juice
1 cup	green tomato chopped
1/2 tsp.	basil
2 tbsp.	butter melted
2 tbsp.	parmesan cheese
1 cup	bread crumbs fine
1 cup	sour cream
1 tbsp.	worcestershire sauce

1. Make pie recipe and prepare pie plate. Add bottom half of pastry to pie plate.

2. Combine all of the remaining ingredients gently in a deep bowl until evenly mixed. Spread evenly into the pie shell.

3. Cover with top half of pie shell.

4. Bake at 375° F for 30-45 minutes, or until crust is golden.

5.* (Optional) When the pie is ready to come out of the oven cover it with freshly grated parmesan cheese and replace in oven until melted.

Lighthouse Spicy Seafood Boil

1 lb.	small mussels in the shell
1 lb.	baby clams
1 lb.	lobster meat
1 lb.	lobster claws in shell
1 lb.	baby scallops
1 lb.	shrimp
2 cups	stewed tomatoes chopped
1 cup	onion diced
1 cup	mushroom sliced
1 cup	celery diced
2 cups	tomato juice
2 tbsp.	garlic minced
1 tsp.	cumin
1 tbsp.	basil
1 tsp.	oregano
1 tsp.	cayenne pepper
1 tsp.	chili pepper
1/4 cup	jalapeno pepper minced
1/4 cup	crushed chilies
4 cups	chicken stock

Salt & pepper to taste.

1. Clean all seafood and set aside.

2. Place all into a large deep pot. Mix well and cover. Let simmer on low for 1 hour, stirring about 6 times during cooking.

3. Serve piping hot with garlic bread or baguette.

* * *

Grand Manan is a 2 hour ferry ride from Blacks Harbour. It is worth the trip to see the lighthouse and to sample some freshly harvested dulse from the region.

Curried Atlantic Salmon Steaks

2 lbs.	salmon steaks
3	eggs
1 tbsp.	garlic minced
4 tsps.	curry powder
1 tsp.	salt
1 tsp.	pepper
1	béchamel sauce recipe page 75.
1/2 tsp.	paprika
1 cup	apple sauce

1. Clean fish and pat dry and set aside.

2. Make egg wash of eggs, garlic, 2 tsps. curry, 1 tsp. of salt & pepper. Mix well. Set aside.

3. Make béchamel sauce and add 2 tsps. of curry, 1/2 tsp. salt, apple sauce and paprika. Stir well and heat over medium heat until hot.

3. Dip fish into egg wash and coat evenly. Fry in a hot pan until crispy all over.

4. Serve salmon steaks on a bed of rice and next to a side salad with the sauce dribbled over both.

* * *

In Queen's County you will find the quaint little town of Gagetown nestled on the shore of the St.John River. It is home to many crafts people and those who treasure a peaceful way of life. Travel on from there to Hampton via the highway system that incorporates toll free ferries to cross the inland water ways.

Fundy Shore Tartar Sauce

1-1/2 cups	mayonnaise
1 cup	relish or gherkin pickles minced
1/4 cup	lemon juice
1 tsp.	garlic minced
1/2 tsp.	white pepper
1 tsp.	olive oil
1 tsp.	mustard
1/4 tsp.	salt
1/4 cup	cider vinegar
1/2 tsp.	dried dill
1/4 tsp.	paprika
1/4 cup	onion minced
1 tsp.	anchovy paste *
1 tsp.	capers minced *

1. Mix all of the above ingredients in a deep bowl until completely smooth and creamy.

2. Let sit in refrigerator for 1 hour so the flavors blend.

3. Serve as a condiment over any fish, with french fries or as a sandwich spread.

Fat Free: Cottage cheese, yogurt or fat free sour cream in place of the mayonnaise.

* Anchovy and capers optional.

* * *

Whale watching is a popular activity for visitors to New Brunswick. The most frequently sighted whales are the Finback, Right, Minke, and Humpback. Tours can be arranged from Campobello Island, Caraquet, Deer Island, Grand Manan Island, Saint John, St. Andrews and St. George.

Periwinkles

2 lbs.	periwinkles
1 recipe	alfredo sauce on page 73, cooled
1/2 cup	parmesan cheese shredded
1 cup	mozzarella cheese shredded

1. Clean periwinkles and place in an escargot bowl or any shallow baking dish.

2. Cover with Alfredo sauce and bake uncovered for 20 minutes at 400° F.

3. Remove from oven, sprinkle parmesan and then mozzarella cheese. Return to oven and broil until cheese is bubbly and melted.

Serve as an appetizer or as a main dish with a side of salad and crusty bread.

* * *

Perth Andover offers some of the best hunting, fishing and wilderness areas to be found anywhere. The Beechwood Hydro Dam nearby offers guided tours of the generating station. Here you can see a fish elevator designed to help Atlantic Salmon over the dam to their spawning waters.

Grilled Tuna

Although N.B. fisherman don't bring home tuna, we still love to serve it. Tuna is a firm fish that lends itself to the barbecue nicely.

1/2 cup	butter
1 tbsp.	cayenne pepper
1 tsp.	garlic powder
1/2 tsp.	salt
1 tsp.	black pepper
2 lbs.	tuna fillets

Lemon or lime wedges (optional).

1. Wash and pat dry tuna fillets and set aside. Melt butter over low heat and add all seasonings.

2. Place tuna onto hot barbecue and baste with butter mixture quite often. Turn over only once and repeat. Cook for 8-10 minutes per side. The fish will be plump and the color will change once cooked.

Salmon Dip

1 cup	herbed or plain cream cheese
1/2 bag	spinach washed & chopped
1 lb.	salmon cooked & cooled
1 tsp.	lemon juice
1 tsp.	soya sauce
1 tbsp.	onion minced
2 tbsp.	red onion minced
1/2 tsp.	dill dried
1/2 tsp.	cayenne pepper

Salt & pepper to taste.

1. Purée all of the ingredients in a blender or food processor until smooth.

2. Place in a serving dish. Cover and chill for 2 hours before using.

Stuffed Barbecue Salmon

1	salmon
4 cups	bread crumbs
1-1/2 cups	onion minced
1/2 cup	red pepper minced
1/4 cup	green pepper minced
2 tbsp.	garlic minced
1/2 cup	almonds ground
1/4 cup	almonds sliced
1/2 cup	apple minced
1/4 cup	butter melted
1/4 cup	lemon juice
1/4 cup	pistachio nuts
Salt & pepper to taste.	

1. Choose a salmon that is big enough to feed your crowd. (about 2 inches in length per person).

2. Clean salmon, remove the head and tail. Next slice it open along the belly and remove the backbone. You can leave head and tail on for decoration if you like.

3. To make stuffing: combine all of the ingredients in a deep bowl, mixing well.

4. Stuff salmon, being certain not to overstuff.

5. Wrap salmon loosely in tinfoil.

6. Cook approximately 2 hours, either in an oven at 350° F or on the upper rack of a barbecue that has reached 350° F.

7. Let salmon sit for 10 minutes before unwrapping to retain the natural moisture.

Spinach Stuffed Cod Florentine

1/2 cup	pistachios *
2 cups	spinach, cleaned & minced
1 tbsp.	onion minced
1 tbsp.	celery minced
1 tbsp.	garlic minced
1 tsp.	chili powder
1/2 tsp.	dill (dried)
1 cup	ricotta or cottage cheese
1 cup	green tomato diced
2 lbs.	cod fish fillets
Salt & pepper to taste.	

1. Place all of the ingredients except for the tomatoes and codfish, into a food processor and blend well.

2. Fold in the diced tomatoes and mix by hand until tomatoes are evenly mixed in. Set aside.

3. Clean fillets and lay flat. Use approx. 1-3 tbsps. of filling per fillet, and roll it up like a log.

4. Place in a shallow baking dish with a 1" space between each fillet.

5. Bake for 20 minutes at 350° F.

Hint: You may like to serve the fish with a sauce like hollandaise, white sauce or a cheese sauce.

* You can use any type of nut you like, pine nuts, almonds, cashews, walnuts, etc.

Fundy Fish Chowder

2 lbs.	white fish cubed
1/2 lb.	salmon cubed
1 cup	baby clams, canned with juice
1 cup	baby shrimp canned or fresh (cleaned)
2 cups	cubed potatoes
1/2 cup	diced carrots
1/8 cup	bacon, crispy & crushed
1/2 cup	red pepper minced
1/2 cup	mushroom minced
1 cup	celery minced
1/2 cup	onion minced
1 tsp.	rosemary rubbed
1 tsp.	black pepper
1 tbsp.	garlic minced
1/2 tsp.	dill dried
1/2 cup	white wine
4 cups	chicken stock
2 cups	evaporated milk
Salt to taste.	

1. Place all of the ingredients in a deep pot . Simmer on low for 1 hour stirring often.

2. Serve with the Maritime Lobster Croissant recipe on page 122, for a soup and sandwich combo that is a classic New Brunswick Dish.

* * *

Kouchibouguac National Park offers the warmest salt water north of Virginia. Swimming, nature walks, biking, and excellent camping facilities await the traveller.

Calamari (Squid)

2 lbs.	cleaned squid
1 cup	chicken stock
1 tsp.	pepper
1 tsp.	cayenne pepper
1 tsp.	chili powder
2 tbsp.	garlic minced
1/4 cup	lemon juice
1 recipe	tempura on page 43.
1/4 cup	clarified butter

1. Clean and cut squid up into little rings.

2. Combine chicken stock, pepper, cayenne pepper, chili powder, garlic, and lemon juice. Soak Calamari for 2 hours in the mixture.

3. Drain liquid off and discard.

4. Dip squid into a tempura and fry in a non-stick frying pan in clarified butter until golden brown.

5. Pat dry on a paper towel and serve.

Hint: Serve as a snack or hors-d'oeuvre or as a main meal with a salad and some rice.

Hint: Serve with dipping sauces like a salsa , sour cream, onion dip, ranch, or Caesar dip.

* * *

Bouctouche is a lovely town with beautiful beaches and the Irving Eco-Centre La Dune de Bouctouche. Stroll the boardwalk and learn about the fragile ecology of the dunes and their preservation. Be sure to visit the interpretation centre where there are lots of fun learning experiences for young and old.

Hearty Lobster Chowder

2 lbs.	cut up raw lobster, cleaned
1 lb.	claws, raw, cleaned, in the shell
2 cups	potatoes diced
1/2 cup	onion minced
3/4 cup	red pepper minced
1 cup	celery minced
1 tsp.	garlic minced
1/4 cup	bacon crispy & minced
1 tsp.	rosemary rubbed
2 tbsp.	parsley
1 tsp.	pepper
1 tsp.	cumin
1 tbsp.	butter * (optional)
1 cup	white wine
2 cups	evaporated milk
3 cups	chicken or vegetable stock
1 cup	sour cream * (optional)
Salt & pepper to taste.	

1. Place all of the ingredients into a large deep stew pot and simmer on low heat for 1 hour stirring often.

* Fat Free: Use skim milk or fat free sour cream and no butter.

* * *

Sea kayaking is an increasingly popular aquatic adventure. St. George, St. Andrews and Bathurst are great spots to visit and to arrange a tour up close and personal with the waters around New Brunswick.

Bay Scallops with Linguine, Dill and Mushrooms

(individual serving)

3/4 cup	cooked pasta
1/2 lb.	scallops cleaned & thinly sliced
1 tbsp.	clarified butter
1 tsp.	garlic minced
1/2 tsp.	dill dried
1 tbsp.	red onion minced
1 cup	mushrooms sliced
1 cup	spinach washed & julienned
Salt & pepper to taste.	

1. Sauté scallops in butter with garlic, dill, red onion, mushrooms, salt & pepper until cooked, about 5 minutes over medium heat.

2. Toss in the pasta and heat till pasta is warmed.

3. Toss in spinach and keep tossing until spinach is heated.

4. Top with fresh grated parmesan cheese and place in a thin line with warm diced tomatoes around the edge of the plate.

Creamy Summer Shrimp Alfredo
(individual serving)

1/2 lb.	raw shrimp
1 cup	cooked pasta
1/2 tsp.	garlic minced
1/4 tsp.	black pepper
1 tsp.	onion minced
1 tsp.	clarified butter
1/4 cup	red pepper diced
1/2 cup	whipping cream
1/2 cup	milk
1/4 cup	parmesan cheese fresh or dried
1/2 tsp.	parsley dried
Dash of salt.	

1. Sauté the shrimp in the butter with garlic , red pepper and onions over medium heat until shrimp are tender. About 5 minutes.

2. Add the pasta, pepper, salt, milk, whipping cream and parsley. Stir well.

3. Bring liquid to a rolling boil and add the cheese. Stir constantly until thickened.

4. Turn off heat. Let sit 2 minutes until mixture thickens.

Fat Free: You can use skim milk and fat reduced cheese but this is a rich dish and a thick liquid like whipping cream is needed. You can use buttermilk which has less fat but it will alter the taste a little. If you make it fat free the mixture will be of a thinner consistency.

Optional: Add 1 tbsp. hot smoked green chili peppers.

Poached Atlantic Salmon

2 lbs.	salmon fillets or steaks
1	lemon sliced in rounds
1 tsp.	salt
1 tsp.	black peppercorns crushed
2 twigs	dill
1 twig	anise
2 stalks	celery
1 tsp.	garlic minced
1 tsp.	rosemary rubbed
4 cups	chicken stock

1. Place all of the ingredients except for salmon into a stock pot, and cover with water until 3/4 full. Bring to a boil.

2. Reduce heat so water stops boiling and maintains a medium heat.

3. Add salmon pushing it under the liquid. Cook for 8 minutes on each side.

4. Drain and serve over a bed of rice with a side dish of sautéed vegetables.

Hint: Goes great over a bed of rice with sautéed vegetables.

Maritime Lobster Croissant

1	croissant
1 tsp.	mayonnaise*
1 tsp.	green onion minced
1/2 tsp.	lemon juice
1 tsp.	mustard
1 tsp.	celery minced
3 oz	lobster, cleaned & chopped
1/4 cup	shredded cheese of choice
1 tbsp.	garlic butter

1. Mix mayonnaise, green onion, lemon juice, mustard, celery, and the lobster all together in a bowl until evenly mixed. Set aside in fridge.

2. Slice the croissant in half and butter insides with garlic butter.

3. Fry buttered side down in a frying pan or buttered side up in the oven under the broiler.

4. Place the lobster mixture on the bottom half of the croissant.

5. Top with shredded cheese.

6. Place under broiler in oven to melt. Top with other half of croissant and serve.

* You can change the mayonnaise to ranch salad dressing, or any other condiment you prefer.

* * *

Shediac is the lobster capital of the world. The Lobster Festival is an opportunity for all to toast this delectable delicacy. Revellers also make time to enjoy the wonderful sand and surf at Parlee Beach.

Picnics & Barbeques

Picnics & Barbeques

Fundy Shore Clam Bake

5 lbs.	raw cleaned clams
25 lbs.	beach rocks
1	shovel
2 lbs.	clean seaweed
1 bundle	wood
1 box	matches
1 large	pot (not a family treasure)
1	beach with good weather
1 group	great friends & family

1. You will need to make a fire pot out of rocks or dig a fire pit. To build a fire pot, collect some large rocks. Place rocks in a circle to form the base of the pot. Place a large flat rock over the top of the circle to hold the clams. Lay seaweed on top. Build up the sides with more rocks. Place the clams on the seaweed, layer more seaweed on top. Or you could dig a pit to hold the firewood. Lay logs across the top of the pit to hold the pot. Layer wet seaweed in the bottom of the pot followed by a layer of clams. Continue layering seaweed and clams until all are in the pit.

2. Light the fire. The clams cook in about 20 minutes with good heat .

3. Eat the clams right out of the shell. For added flavor put a couple of lemons or oranges, pepper and/or some beer or wine in with the clams.

Hint: Don't forget the melted butter for dipping. Add crusty bread, corn on the cob, apples, and cheese, to round out the meal. Make it a beach barbecue!

Why not dig your own clams ...nothing will taste better than your own harvest. Just ask around to find where the best digging place is and then head off with a few buckets.

Sweet Grilled Shrimp Pita

6	tiger shrimp, large
1	onion small, cut into thin rounds
1/2 cup	commercial sweet'n sour sauce
1	pita pocket
2 tsps.	mayonnaise
1/4 cup	shredded lettuce
1/4 cup	swiss cheese, finely shredded
Salt & pepper to taste.	

1. Clean shrimp. Dip shrimp and onion rings into the sweet'n sour sauce to coat.

2. Place on grill.

3. Cook for 10 minutes or until shrimp are completely pink in colour.

4. While it is cooking peel open the pita shell and cut in half, stuff one side inside the other.

5. Brush insides of pita with mayonnaise. Remove onion and shrimp from grill once cooked and stuff into pita.

6. Cover with cheese and lettuce.

Goes great with a nice summery salad of greens.

Summertime Cold Fruit Salad

3 apples	Granny Smith or Macintosh
2 pears	Anjou
1 cup	strawberries
1 banana	sliced
1/2 cup	maraschino cherry juice
1/2 cup	lemon juice
1 litre	cream, whipped cream, or ice cream

1. Clean and slice all fruit into bite size pieces. In a large bowl combine all fruit, add the cherry and lemon juices.

2. Stir but be gentle so as not to break or bruise the fruit. Let sit in the refrigerator for 2 hours before using. Serve with light cream or whipped cream.

* Makes a nice topping for ice cream as well.

Summer Picnic Potato Vegetable Salad

5 lbs.	potatoes, cooked, cooled & mashed
2 cups	mixed green peas & carrots, canned
1 apple	diced small
1 cup	corn
1 cup	onion minced
1/2 cup	celery minced
1 tsp.	garlic minced
6	eggs hard boiled and mashed
1 cup	mayonnaise
1/2 cup	ranch salad dressing
1 tsp.	parsley
Salt & pepper to taste.	

1. Mix all together and spread into casserole dish. Keep in fridge until ready to serve.

Grilled Lemon Trout

1	large trout whole (cleaned)
2	lemons sliced round
1/2 cup	lemon juice
Salt & pepper to taste.	

1. Pat dry the inside of the fish.

2. Sprinkle the inside with salt and pepper.

3. Place the sliced lemons evenly throughout the cavity of the fish.

4. Wrap with tinfoil so the head and tail are sticking out and poke a few holes in the foil so it can breathe.

5 . Bake on the barbecue. Approximately 10 minutes per inch of length.

6. Let sit 5 minutes before opening.

7. Remove foil and lemon pieces, sprinkle with 1/2 cup of lemon juice as soon as you unwrap it and then slice and serve.

* * *

New Brunswick is criss crossed by many rivers and streams. Hidden within their fresh waters are speckled trout, every fisherman has their favorite spot.

Shish Kebabs

New Brunswick's delicious shish kebabs are fun for summer time treats from the sea & make wonderful additions to any skewer.

Make sure to soak all wooden skewers in water for 1 hour before using. This reduces the chance that your stick may catch on fire in the barbecue.

All food bits should be bite size, clean and raw.

Space food bits onto skewer evenly apart for good even cooking and baste while cooking or marinate before cooking.

There are no set rules. Your guests can make their own if they choose.

Fish Shish Kebabs

Use chunks of white fish,* scallops and shrimp. Space with red onion chunks, green peppers, cherry tomatoes, pineapple chunks, or apple wedges. Baste using lemon juice, pineapple sauce, apple sauce, or barbecue sauce.

* White fish eg. cod, halibut, boston blue, haddock, sword fish, etc.

Pineapple Chicken Shish Kebabs

Sauce

1 cup	crushed pineapple
1/2 cup	applesauce
1 tbsp.	garlic minced
1 tbsp.	soya sauce
1 tbsp.	olive oil

1. Mix ingredients for sauce & marinate chicken in it for 2 hours in the refrigerator.

2. Drain juice and reserve it. Boil juice for 10 minutes. Set aside.

3. Place boneless, skinless, chicken breasts cut in 1-1/2 inch chunks spaced with chunks of sweet yellow and red peppers, mushrooms, pineapple chunks, green tomato wedges and cherry tomatoes on the skewer.

4. While cooking baste with the boiled sauce. Cook till tender.

Steak Shish Kebabs

Marinade

1 tsp.	mint
1 tsp.	oyster sauce
1 tbsp.	soya sauce
1 tbsp.	olive oil
1/2 cup	barbecue sauce
1 tbsp.	garlic minced
1/2 cup	vinegar

1. Mix all ingredients for marinade well and toss over meat stirring so as all meat gets coated.

2. Marinate 2 hours in refrigerator. Drain liquid and discard.

3. Place meat on skewers spaced with onions, cherry tomatoes, mushrooms, and sweet green peppers, and grill until tender.

3 lbs. Steak	cut into thin strips
1 pint	pearl onions
1 pint	cherry tomatoes
1 pint	small mushrooms
2 cups	green pepper (1" chunks)

Vegetable Shish Kebabs

Suggested vegetables:

cherry tomatoes red or green

red onions

sweet onions

sweet peppers in chunks

pineapple wedges or chunks

apple wedges

baby potatoes

mushrooms

asparagus

zucchini

eggplant

1. Slide onto skewers. Place on the grill and baste with barbecue sauce, honey garlic sauce, or a salad dressing, even try pineapple sauce.

* * *

The International Appalachian Trail continues from Mount Katahdin in Baxter State Park, Maine to Perth Andover in New Brunswick. It ventures onto Mount Carleton and the Restigouche River before taking the traveller onto Quebec at Matapedia.

Vegetable Grilled Pocket for 1

1/2	medium red bell pepper, sliced
1/2	medium yellow bell pepper, sliced
4 ozs.	mushrooms, sliced
1	medium onion , quarterd
1/2 cup	Kraft Italian Salad Dressing
1/4 cup	shredded cheese(any flavour) optional

1. Dip all of the vegetables into the salad dressing and place on hot grill on top rack and close lid.

2. Turn once during cooking process.

3. Cook until desired tenderness or for 10 minutes.

4. Brush a pita pocket with water and place on grill. Do not let pita get crispy just warm it.

5. Stuff vegetables into pita and top with shredded cheese of choice.

Barbecue Roasted Vegetables & Fruit

Vegetables & Fruit:

potatoes*	green or red tomatoes
carrots*	pineapple
onions	green peppers
leeks	red peppers
mushrooms	hot peppers
eggplant	apples
peaches	apricots
1 tbsp.	butter melted
1 tsp.	garlic minced

1. Cut vegetables / fruit into chunks.

2. Using a double thickness of tinfoil place vegetables / fruit on half of the sheet.

3. Add melted butter, garlic and salt & pepper to taste.

4. Fold over tinfoil, seal edges, place on upper tray of barbecue.

5. Close lid on barbecue and cook for 15 minutes before checking them. Check and continue cooking until tender.

* Maybe make an envelope for the soft and one for the hard vegetables.

Picnic Time Macaroni Salad

1/4 cup	onion minced
1/4 cup	celery minced
1/2 cup	commercial ranch salad dressing
1 cup	mayonnaise
1 tbsp	lemon juice
1/4 cup	sour cream
1 tsp.	black pepper
1 tsp.	cayenne pepper
1 tsp.	parsley
1 tsp.	garlic powder
4 cups	pasta of choice, cooked & cooled
1/2 cup	shredded spinach per person
1 cup	yellow pepper, diced *

1. Mix all of the above ingredients well until smooth and evenly coated, except for the pasta and spinach.

2. Place 1/2 cup of shredded spinach as a bed for the salad, on each plate.

3. On each bed of spinach place a portion of the Pasta salad.

* For an added flare with color top off each person's plate with 1 tbsp. diced yellow pepper.

* * *

Approximately 130 kilometres / 80 Miles from Riviére-du-Loup in Quebec is Edmundston, New Brunswick. There is a hiking / cycling trail there called Le Petit Terris. It traverses fields and forests, along the Saint John River and past lake fronts. Go in early August and celebrate the unique Brayonne Heritage at Foire Brayonne. The heritage of the French speaking people of this region is distinct from that of the Acadians.

Seared Steak Grillwich

4 oz	marinating sirloin steak
1/2 cup	mushrooms, sliced
1/4	green bell pepper in one piece
4	1/4 inch thick onion slices
1/4 cup	shredded cheddar *
2 tbsps.	olive oil
1 tbsp.	basalmic vinegar
1 tsp.	soya sauce
1 tsp.	worcestershire sauce
1	pita pocket
Salt & pepper to taste.	

1. Cut steak into thin strips.

2. Mix in a deep bowl the worcestershire sauce, soya sauce, vinegar, and olive oil.

3. Toss in steak strips and vegetables. Add salt and pepper to taste.

4. Marinate for 15 minutes.

5. Place on upper rack of grill, being very careful to lay them out so they do not fall down through the grill lines.

6. Close lid and grill meat for 15 minutes.

7. Warm pita on grill.

8. Stuff pita with steak and vegetables.

9. Top with shredded cheddar.

* Optional.

Summer Fresh Salad

1 head	romaine lettuce broken into pieces
1/2 cup	almonds toasted
1/2 cup	mandarin oranges, juice reserved
3/4 cup	red onion diced small
1 cup	olive oil
1/4 cup	red wine vinegar
1/4 cup	white sugar
1/4 cup	cold water

1. In large bowl place lettuce, almonds and oranges, stir well and set aside.

2. In food processor mix onions, oil, vinegar, juice from oranges, sugar and water until frothy (about 4 minutes).

3. Pour over salad, stir and serve.

Chicken & Mushroom B'Bque Pocket

4 ozs.	chicken breast, sliced into 4 slices
1/2 cup	barbecue sauce
1/2 cup	mushrooms, halved
2 tsps.	mayonnaise
1/4 cup	mozzarella, shredded
1	pita pocket

Salt & pepper to taste.

1. Grill chicken and mushrooms until desired tenderness.

2. Smother with barbecue sauce and cook 2 more minutes.

3. Coat inside of pita with mayonnaise and add chicken and mushrooms. Top with cheese and enjoy.

Barbecued Grilled Halibut

1 tsp.	salt
1 tsp.	white pepper
1 tbsp.	garlic minced
1/4 cup	onion minced
1/4 cup	lemon juice
1 cup	commercial plum sauce
1 pint	cherry tomatoes cut into quarters
2 lbs.	halibut steaks

1. Wash fish, set aside.

2. Mix salt, pepper, garlic, onion, lemon juice, plum sauce, and cherry tomatoes in a shallow dish.

3. Place fish in sauce and marinate overnight in the refrigerator in an airtight container or bag for 2 hours.

4. Reserve marinade.

5. Wrap the fish in foil and cook on the barbecue about 10 minutes per side.

6. While the fish cooks, boil marinade to reduce it for a sauce to serve over the fish.

Sweet'n Sour Barbecue Shrimp

2 lbs.	raw large shrimp, shelled & deveined
1 cup	Kraft Italian salad dressing
1/4 cup	brown sugar
2 cups	crushed pineapple
1 tbsp.	garlic
Salt & pepper to taste.	

1. Mix all of the above ingredients in a deep bowl except the shrimp and set aside.

2. Place cleaned shrimp in marinade and soak for 1/2 hour.

3. Remove shrimp from marinade and reserve the liquid.

4. Boil the marinade to cook any raw fish juice. Reduce by one third over medium heat.

5. Place shrimp on the barbecue and baste the shrimp constantly with the marinade until cooked, about 5 minutes per shrimp turning once during cooking.

Caesar Chicken Salad

1 head	romaine lettuce cut into bite size pieces
2 lg.	chicken breasts grilled & cooled
1/2 cup	lemon juice
1/2 cup	apple cider vinegar
2 tbsp.	garlic minced
1 tsp.	oregano dried
1/8 cup	parmesan cheese, thinly shaved

1. Grill chicken and season with salt & pepper, let cool and cut into bite size chunks or strips. Set aside.

2. In large salad bowl place lettuce and chicken breast and set aside.

3. Salad dressing: mix lemon juice, vinegar, garlic and oregano in a deep bowl.

4. Pour salad dressing over top of salad and serve.

Garnish with shaved fresh parmesan cheese.

* * *

Birdwatchers from around the world have descended upon Marys Point in Albert Country in August to see tens of thousands of semi-palmated sandpipers and other birds. The birds are attracted to the salt marshes.

Fruity Summer Orange Dessert

2 cups	orange sections (seedless fresh or canned)
1 cup	yogurt or puréed ricotta or cottage cheese
1/2 cup	orange juice
1/4 cup	orange flavored brandy or liquor
1 tsp.	vanilla extract
2 cups	ice cream, sherbert or whipped cream
1/4 cup	melted milk or dark chocolate chips

1. Lay a 1/2 cup of orange sections in a spiral fashion onto a dessert plate and set aside.

2. In a deep bowl mix the yogurt or cheese with orange juice, brandy, and vanilla until smooth.

3. Pour over fruit, top with ice cream, sherbert or whipped cream.

4. Drizzle with chocolate.

Serves 4

Avocado Shrimp Sandwich

1/4 lb.	Shrimp, cooked or canned
1/2	ripe avocado mashed
4 slices	green tomato, thinly cut
1 slice	swiss cheese
2 slices	lightly toasted bread of choice
2 tsps.	sandwich condiment
Pepper to taste.	

1. Spread condiment on one slice of toasted bread, spread half of the avocado, sprinkle with pepper.

2. Arrange shrimp on top of avocado mixture, top with tomato slices, cheese, other half of the avocado mix and then the other slice of bread. Slice and serve.

Grilled Portabello Mushrooms

Steak, mushrooms and a little red wine finish off an idyllic day at the beach.

1/2 cup	olive oil
2 tbsp.	garlic minced
1 tbsp.	black peppercorns, cracked
1/2 tsp.	salt
1/4 cup	lemon juice
1/4 tsp.	tarragon
4 full	portabello mushrooms

1. Clean and slice mushrooms, set aside.

2. Make a marinade of olive oil, garlic, pepper, salt, lemon juice, and tarragon. Stir well. Pour marinade over mushrooms and let sit for 10 minutes.

3. Drain, grill for 15 minutes, flipping once, baste with marinade.

Miramichi Salmon Spit

You've just caught a prized salmon and can't wait to sample it. Try this rustic cooking method right on the shore or hop in the car and head for the nearest oven or barbecue.

1/2 lb.	butter
1 tsp.	salt
1 tsp.	pepper
1/2 tsp.	dill dried
1 tbsp.	lemon juice
10 lb.	salmon (cleaned)
1 meter	cheesecloth

1. This is a salmon cooked whole or halved lengthwise on a wooden slab on the beach in front of a fire.

2. Slice the fish lengthwise along the belly. Clean and place onto a thin flat wide splint of clean wood.

3. Wrap the salmon in a double layer of cheesecloth and then rub both sides with buttered mixture.

4. For buttered mixture, mix butter, salt, pepper, dill, and lemon juice in a bowl until smooth.

5. Tie salmon onto slab and place into sand. Place the stick well into the sand for support so that the salmon is leaning or hanging towards the fire. Cook until tender. This may vary in time depending on the intensity of the heat and the thickness of the fish, anywhere from 1-4 hrs.

* * *

The Miramichi River is world renowned for its salmon. The river attracts anglers from near and far including the very famous who enjoy the quiet solitude of the rod and reel, and hopefully the fish.

Fresh Seaweed Wrapped Atlantic Salmon

1 bunch	beach seaweed cleaned
10 lb.	salmon cleaned
2 tbsps.	butter
1/4 cup	lemon juice
Salt & pepper.	

1. Sprinkle salmon inside and out with salt and pepper.

2. Rub butter inside the fish.

3. Sprinkle fish all over with lemon juice.

4. Wrap loosely in seaweed until completely covered.

5. Bake over an open campfire, barbecue. (Approximately 2 hours in 300° F heat).

6. Unwrap and serve.

* * *

The St. John River is a world class waterway. The beauty of the river and its' shore can be seen along approx. 685 kilometres / 420 miles of its journey from Saint John to Saint Jacques, from the Bay of Fundy to the Quebec border.

Cold Seafood Pasta Salad

6 cups	pasta, cooked & cooled
2 cups	* seafood, cooked & cooled
1 cup	mayonnaise
1/4 cup	lemon juice
1/4 cup	olive oil
1/4 cup	red vinegar
1 tbsp.	garlic minced
1 tsp.	dill dried
1 cup	celery sliced
1/4 cup	onion minced
1 cup	red pepper diced
1 cup	yellow pepper diced
1 cup	fresh garden green peas
1/4 cup	red onion minced
Salt and pepper to taste.	

1. Mix all ingredients except for the pasta in a large deep mixing bowl until mixed evenly.

2. Toss in pasta and mix until all pasta is coated.

3. Chill for 2 hours before serving.

4. Serve on a bed of greens such as spinach, romaine, leaf lettuce or iceberg.

* Seafood: try scallops, shrimp, salmon, pollock, or a combination of either.

* * *

Cape Tormentine is situated on the New Brunswick side of the Confederation Bridge. This 13 kilometre structure spans the Northumberland Strait and is the longest bridge in the western hemisphere.

Cool Down Ice Cream Cookies

1 recipe	chocolate chip cookies page 183.
1 litre	favorite ice cream
2 cups	chocolate chips, any flavor.

1. Bake chocolate chip cookie as recipe says but shape them so they are about 2 inches round in diameter.

2. Cool cookies.

3. On a cookie sheet lay out cookies with their face down on the cookie sheet. Cover each cookie with a spoonful of ice cream and shape it so it fits the same shape as the cookie. Press another cookie face up on top of the ice cream.

4. You must work quickly as the ice cream melts fast. Put cookies stuffed with ice cream into the freezer to get hard.

5. Melt chocolate chips in a double boiler or microwave until soft.

6. Remove cookies from freezer and dip half or all of the cookie into the chocolate mixture.

7. Place onto a very lightly greased cookie sheet and return to freezer right away.

8. Wrap individually and store in freezer or serve.

* * *

Magnetic Hill not only offers a waterslide park and a zoo, but also the opportunity to defy nature. You can sit in your car and coast uphill. It is an intriguing phenomenon.

Slow Roasted Herbed Salmon

4 large	salmon steaks
8 sprigs	anise
8 sprigs	coriander
1/2 cup	garlic butter melted
1/4 cup	lemon juice
Salt & pepper to taste.	

1. Clean steaks and pat dry, season with salt & pepper. Set aside.

2. Gather a sprig of anise and coriander for each steak. Tie to steak with kitchen string.

3. Brush salmon with melted garlic butter on both sides. Lay steak on grill.

4. Drizzle over each steak, 2 tbsps. of lemon juice. Make a hat made of foil over each steak so as to create a little oven over each one.

5. Grill for 30 minutes on 325° F.

* * *

Campbellton's Restigouche River is well known for salmon fishing. The town celebrates this delicacy with a salmon festival each June.

Party Mix

8 cups	shreddies cereal
4 cups	pretzels
1 lb.	salted peanuts
4 cups	cheerios cereal
1/2 cup	melted butter
1 tbsp.	garlic salt

Optional: add bugles or cheese nips if desired

1. Melt butter and add garlic salt, and mix well. Place rest of the ingredients into a large deep bowl and coat with melted butter.

2. Place onto a cookie sheet and bake at 200° F for 1 hour turning occasionally.

Hint: You can change the flavor by using popcorn seasoning powders usually found in bulk stores. Try flavors like onion, ranch, barbecue, etc.

Candied Nuts

1	egg white
1/4 cup	brown sugar
1 tsp.	chili powder
1 tbsp.	soya sauce
2 tbsp.	butter melted
4 cups	mixed nuts

1. Mix egg white, brown sugar, chili, soya, and melted butter in a deep bowl until well blended. About 5 minutes with whisk by hand.

2. Add in nuts and swish them around to coat.

3. Drain and place on a cookie sheet. Bake at 375° F for 10 minutes or until nuts are just lightly toasted.

Harvest Oat Bars

1 cup	brown sugar
1/2 cup	butter or margarine
1/2 cup	corn syrup
3 tsp.	vanilla
1 tsp.	salt
4 cups	rolled quick minute oats

1. Place all of the above ingredients into a pot and cook over medium heat until oatmeal is cooked. About 5 minutes.

2. Place mixture into a rectangle pan and bake for 15 minutes at 350° F. Let cool and cut into bar shapes.

Hint: For a frosting, melt 1/2 cup peanut butter and 1 cup of chocolate chips over medium heat or in microwave till smooth and mixed evenly. Spread over top of cookies when still slightly warm.

Traditional
Peanut Butter Cookies

1/2 cup	butter or margarine
1/2 cup	peanut butter
1/2 cup	white sugar
1/2 cup	brown sugar
1	egg
1-1/3 cups	flour
1/2 tsp.	baking powder
1/2 cup	nuts crushed* (optional)

1. Cream the butter, peanut butter, and sugars together.

2. Add the egg, and mix in the rest of the ingredients until even.

3. Roll into small balls and press with fork onto an ungreased cookie sheet.

4. Bake at 350° F for 10 minutes, then remove and cool.

Hint: For a different flare try adding 1/2 cup of crushed nuts of choice to the recipe or dusting each cookie with crushed nuts before baking.

* * *

Rockwood Park in Saint John is the largest municipal park in Canada. Sprawling over 2200 acres it offers swimming, paddle boats, canoes, fishing, golf, hiking trails, horseback riding and even a zoo. In the winter it is popular for cross country skiing and for skating at Lily Lake.

Grandma's Bran Muffins

2-1/2 cups	white sugar
1/2 cup	molasses
1/2 tsp.	salt
2 tsps.	baking soda
4	eggs
5-1/2 cups	flour
5 cups	sour milk
1-1/2 cups	vegetable oil
2 cups	dried fruit or nuts (optional)
3 cups	bran flakes
2 cups	natural bran

1. In a deep bowl, mix all of the wet ingredients first, and then add the dry. Beat until smooth.

2. Place muffin paper liners in the pan, or lightly grease each muffin cavity.

3. Bake at 400° F for 15 minutes until center springs back .

4. Makes two dozen.

Finishing Touches

Sweet Poached Pears

1 cup	lemon juice
1 lemon	sliced round
1	cinnamon stick
6	cloves
1	orange sliced round
1/4 cup	maraschino cherry juice
1 tsp.	black cracked peppercorns
1 cup	white wine
2 cups	water
6	pears

1. Make a poaching liquid from the ingredients above except pears by placing them in a shallow stock pot and bringing them to a boil.

2. While stock is boiling, peel pears, use Bosc or Anjou pears (or any other firm pear). Peel the pear and flatten the bottom by cutting it off so it sits flat. Partially core it out through the bottom to remove the stem about 2 inches deep.

3. When poaching stock has boiled, reduce the heat to medium and submerge the pears into the liquid.

4. Cover and cook 10 minutes on medium heat.

5. Remove pears and place nicely on dessert plate.

6. Garnish with orange slices, maraschino cherries, whipped cream, or ice cream.

Hint: Serve warm or cold or serve onto a plate with pudding.

Apricot Treasure Fruit Cake

1 cup	butter
1-1/4 cups	white sugar
1/4 cup	apricot brandy
1 tbsp.	almond extract
1/2 cup	margarine
6	eggs
3 cups	flour
1/2 tsp.	baking powder
1/4 tsp.	salt
1/2 tsp.	ginger
1 tsp.	allspice
1 tsp.	dry instant coffee granules
2-1/2 cups	white raisins
2 cups	dried apricots minced
2 cups	dates chopped
1 cup	mixed fruit and cherries or just cherries
2/3 cup	almonds slivered

1. Prepare 2 months before needed as it has to cure. Makes 2 loaves.

2. Cream butter, white sugar, apricot brandy, almond extract, margarine, eggs all together in a deep bowl until smooth.

3. Mix all fruit, that is the raisins, apricots, dates, and mixed fruit in a bowl with 1 cup of flour until all fruit is coated well. The flour will absorb the stickiness of the fruit so it can become suspended in the cake batter. Set aside.

4. Add all remaining ingredients into the creamed mixture and mix thoroughly.

5. Add fruit to cake batter and stir, mixture will become very stiff.

6. Set cake batter aside.

7. Line loaf pans with brown paper bag, then butter it slightly, then layer again with parchment paper and re-grease with butter lightly.

8. Place half of cake batter into each loaf pan.

9. Bake at 275° F for 2 1/2 hours.

10. Once cooled brush each loaf with 4 oz of apricot brandy and let air dry for 4 hrs then wrap in tinfoil and store in dry cool place covered air tight for 6 weeks minimum.

11. Each week brush each loaf with 1/2 oz of apricot brandy and rewrap and store.

Hint: This loaf is high in alcohol content so it is not recommended for children.

Hint: This cake is wonderful for a Christmas tea party or for any tea party.

Hint: Goes well with the home made hot chocolate on page 168.

* * *

New Brunswickers are informal, friendly people. It is common to be entertained around the kitchen table with a steaming mug of tea or coffee and a delicious cake.

Wintertime Hot Cross Buns

1 recipe	soft sweet bread page 158.
2 tsp.	cinnamon
1/2 tsp.	allspice
1/2 tsp.	crushed cloves
1 cup	white raisins
1 cup	mixed dried fruit (optional)
3 tbsp.	cold water
1-1/2 cups	icing sugar

1. You will make this recipe the same as the Soft Sweet Bread recipe except first you will add the cinnamon, allspice, clove, raisins, and dried fruit to the warm milk mixture and then follow the recipe as is but shape into buns instead of loaves.

2. Bake as recipe calls for.

3. While buns are baking, make a glaze out of cold water and icing sugar. Mix both ingredients until smooth and set aside.

4. Once buns have slightly cooled drizzle glaze over top.

Hint: Any dried fruit can be used, apricots, papaya, dates, pineapple, cherries, mixed peel, apple slices, ginger, etc. A combination of any may be used as well.

Hint: This is a nice afternoon bread with a hot pot of coffee for a light snack or a wonderful dessert after a Sunday dinner.

* * *

Caraquet was founded in 1758. Visitors will come away with a taste of all that the Acadian culture has to offer. Nestled on the coast, this picturesque town has beaches, great shops, excellent food, crafts, theaters, festivals and museums. In particular the Acadian Historical Village is a must see.

Soft Sweet Bread

1 cup	milk
2 tsp.	salt
1/4 cup	soft shortening or butter
1/2 cup	luke warm water
2 tsp.	white sugar
2	envelopes fast rising dry yeast
2	eggs
7 - 7-1/2 cups	flour
1/2 cup	white sugar
3/4 cup	cold water

1. Grease bread pans and set aside.

2. Preheat oven to 350° F.

3. Scald the milk in a pot with 1/2 cup of the sugar, salt, cold water and shortening. Cool till it is lukewarm.

4. Using the 1/2 cup lukewarm water, stir in 2 tsp. sugar and sprinkle with the yeast and let rise for 10 minutes.

5. Add the lukewarm milk mixture to the yeast mixture, and stir well.

6. Add the eggs and 3-1/2 cups of the flour and mix until smooth and elastic like.

7. Work in the rest of the flour bit by bit, until all is used. Sit dough in a greased bowl and cover with a piece of lightly greased waxed paper.

8. Let rise in a warm place until it has doubled its own size.

9. Punch dough down and reknead for a few minutes .

10. Shape as desired, place into baking pan. Let dough re-rise for 20 minutes.

11. Bake at 350° F for 30 minutes.

Hint: The best days to make bread are on sunny clear days as if the day is overcast the air pressure will not let your bread rise.

Hint: Do not have the yeast water too hot or too cold. The yeast is what makes the bread rise. Warm water will activate the yeast but not cook it. Also if the water is too warm it will require more flour as it will make a stickier dough.

Hint: Do not over knead the dough as this makes for a tough bread.

Hint: If you make your loaf into 3 little sections per loaf the bread is shaped to handle cutting better. When you bake a loaf in one solid shape it tends not to have strength against cutting.

Rich Chocolate Fudge

1-1/2 cups	nuts roasted
16 (1-oz) squares	chocolate (semi sweet)
1 can	sweetened condensed milk
2 tsps.	vanilla

1. Lightly grease a 8" x 8" pan, and set aside.

2. Melt chocolate with milk in the microwave on high for 2-3 minutes. Stir till creamy and smooth.

3. Add the vanilla and nuts and mix well but quickly.

4. Spread into lightly greased pan. Chill till firm.

Hint: Serve on a plate surrounded by wild flowers for an attractive display.

* * *

The purple violet is the provincial flower of New Brunswick.

Wacky Chocolate Cake

1 cup	white sugar
1-1/2 cups	white flour
1/4 cup	cocoa
1 tsp.	baking soda
1 tbsp.	vinegar
1/3 cup	vegetable oil
1 tbsp.	vanilla
1 cup	cold water

1. Sift all the dry ingredients together into the pan you want to bake the cake in.

2. Place all the liquid ingredients together in one bowl and give a quick stir.

3. Then add all the liquids at once to the dry ingredients.

4. Stir by hand until mixture is smooth, about 5 minutes.

5. Bake at 350° F for 35 minutes.

Try your favorite frosting recipe or the glaze recipe on page 189.

Easy Microwave Chocolate Fudge

3-1/2 cups	icing sugar
1/2 cup	cocoa
1/4 cup	evaporated milk
1/2 cup	butter
1 tsp.	vanilla
1/2 cup	chopped nuts of choice (optional)
Dash of salt.	

1. Lightly grease a 8" x 8" pan with butter. Set aside.

2. Sift the icing sugar and cocoa together.

3. In a microwaveable bowl place the dry ingredients, add milk and butter, that has been chopped into little cubes.

4. Do not stir. Place mixture as is into the microwave for 2-1/2 minutes.

Remove.

5. Working quickly, add vanilla and nuts and stir until smooth. Spread into prepared pan.

6. Place in refrigerator to set.

Hint: This is a soft fudge so keep it cool before serving. Leave at room temperature for 10 minutes before serving for optimum flavor.

* * *

In 1906 the first chocolate bar was born in St. Stephen at the Ganong Candy Factory. Chocolate lovers will enjoy a tour of the Chocolate Museum and may be able to time their visit with the summer Chocolate Festival.

Decadent Death by Chocolate

1 recipe	chocolate cake page 160
1 cup	commercial hot fudge sauce
1 recipe	chocolate frosting
1 recipe	whipped cream page 170

1. Open jar of hot fudge sauce.

2. Make the chocolate cake recipe on page 160, prepare in a pan as per directions. Swirl the chocolate fudge sauce over top and cut through with a knife. Bake as usual.

3. When the cake is cooled, frost the cake with your favorite chocolate frosting recipe.

Variations:

1. Hint: Decorate with shaved curls of chocolate.

2. After frosting the cake, pour cooled hot fudge sauce over top and just have whipped cream on hand.

3. Black Forest Cake: Add 1 cup of cherries (canned or fresh) into the cake batter before baking, or scoop out a hole in the top of the cake after baking and fill with cherries. Leave the cherries open to view (ie. do not frost). Drizzle on some fudge sauce.

4. Individual servings: place a small portion in a bowl. Pour hot fudge sauce on top and then some whipped cream.

Relaxing Coffee Time Cake

Cake:

1/2 cup	shortening
1 cup	white sugar
2	eggs
1/3 cup	molasses
1/4 tsp.	baking soda
1 tsp.	cinnamon
1/2 tsp.	nutmeg
1/4 tsp.	ground cloves
1/2 tsp.	salt
2-1/4 cups	flour
2 tsps.	baking powder
2/3 cup	milk

Frosting:

2-1/2 cups	icing sugar
1/2 cup	flour
1 tsp.	vanilla
1/2 cup	plus 2 tbsps. of softened butter
2 tbsp.	evaporated milk
dash	salt

1. Cream 1 cup sugar and 1/2 cup shortening, add eggs, beat well, add the molasses and beat again.

2. Sift baking soda, cinnamon, nutmeg, cloves, 1/2 tsp. salt, 2-1/4 cups flour, 2 tsps. baking powder.

3. Add to creamed mixture alternating with the milk.

4. Bake in a greased 9" x 13" pan at 350° F for 35 - 40 minutes.

5. While cake is cooking make your frosting. Mix all frosting ingredients in a deep bowl until smooth and spread onto cake.

Classic White Scratch Cake

1/2 cup	shortening
3/4 cup	white sugar
2	eggs
1 tsp.	vanilla
1-3/4 cups	white flour
2 tsp.	baking powder
1/4 tsp.	cream of tartar
1/2 tsp.	salt
2/3 cup	milk

1. Cream shortening, sugar and eggs. Add all rest of the ingredients alternating with the milk.

2. Mix well until smooth either by machine for 5 minutes or by hand for 8 minutes.

3. Bake in a greased and floured 9" x 13" pan at 350° F for 40-60 minutes, or in muffin tins for 25-30 minutes.

4. Frost cake with your favorite frosting.

Hint: You can frost cake with whipped cream and then fresh mixed berries.

Hint: Make 2 layers and spread the center with home made jam. Then frost with frosting or whipped cream.

Cherry Jubilee Shortbread

1 cup	butter
2 cups	white flour
3/4 cup	brown sugar
1 egg	yolk
1 tbsp.	maraschino cherry juice
1 cup	maraschino cherries

1. Cream sugar and butter with cherry juice, and egg yolk until smooth.

2. Stir in flour until you have a stiff crumbly dough. Knead but be careful not to toughen dough.

3. Roll into little balls and then flatten them. Place them on an ungreased cookie sheet.

4. Place half of a cherry in the center of each cookie and bake 10-12 minutes at 350° F.

Variation: Cherries maybe minced and added to the mixture for a more flavorful cherry taste and look. Use 1/4 cup minced cherries and increase the flour by 2 tbsps. to absorb the extra moisture.

Caramel Sauce

1 can	sweetened condensed milk
1	large deep pot

1. Place the unopened can of milk in a pot of cold water. Bring to a boil. Let it simmer on low heat for 30 minutes.

2. Let sit to cool 12 hours at room temperature.

Use as a caramel sauce over ice cream, cakes or pies.

or

25	caramels
1/2 cup	whipping cream or evaporated can milk

1. Place all into a heavy bottomed pot and stir constantly over medium heat until melted smooth.

2. Let cool at room temperature and then store in refrigerator.

Can be used as a topping for ice cream, desserts, cakes, and pies.

Angelic White Cake

2 cups	white flour
1/2 tsp.	salt
2 tsp.	cream of tartar
1 tsp.	baking soda
1/2 cup	butter (room temperature)
1 cup	milk
2	eggs
1 cup	white sugar
1 tsp.	vanilla

1. Sift flour, sugar, salt, cream of tartar and baking soda together in a deep bowl.

2. Cut in butter.

3. When well blended add milk, vanilla and eggs.

4. Beat well until mixture is smooth about 5 minutes.

5. Pour into a greased and floured 8" x 8" baking dish and bake for 20-25 minutes on 400° F.

6. Let cool for 5 minutes and then remove from pan and cool.

7. Frost once cooled if desired.

Mmmmmmmm!!! Homemade Hot Chocolate

1-1/2 cup	evaporated can milk
3 cups	water
1/2 cup	instant chocolate powder mix (not cocoa)

1. Mix all well over medium heat until hot or heat up in a bowl in the microwave.

2. Serve piping hot. Topped with ice cream or whipped cream and chocolate shavings.

* * *

From long before famous Speed Skater Charlie Gorman carved up the ice at Lily Lake to the sound of St. Mary's Band, New Brunswickers' have loved to skate. When the conditions are right you can travel for miles along the Kennebecasis River waving to brave souls who drive across the ice roads on the river.

Cranberry Treasure Pots

1 recipe	muffin batter, but omit the fruit
1/2 tsp.	cinnamon
dash	nutmeg
2 cups	cranberries
2 tbsps.	flour
1/2 cup	brown sugar

1. Mix batter as normal and set aside.

2. Coat berries with flour and then add nutmeg and cinnamon.

3. Add berries to batter mixture and stir gently until all is blended.

4. Place batter into lightly greased muffin pan and top each muffin with 1/2 tsp. of brown sugar.

5. Bake at 350° F for 20 – 45 minutes until center springs back or cake tester is clean.

Homespun Whipped Cream

4 cups	whipping cream
1/2 cup	icing sugar
1 tsp.	vanilla

1. Using electric mixer, beat the ingredients until stiff peaks are formed.

2. Keep in the refrigerator. You may need to re-beat before using if stored for awhile.

* * *

When it comes time to get a Christmas tree, many tree farms offer a traditional family outing. You can ride out to find a tree and a wagon and then return to the cabin to warm up, with delicious hot chocolate and gingerbread. Both taste better with a dollop of whip cream.

Peanut Brittle

2 cups	unsalted peanuts, cashews or pecans
2 cups	white sugar
1 cup	light colored corn syrup
1/3 cup	water
2 tbsp.	butter (no substitute)
1 tsp.	baking soda
1 tsp.	vanilla

1. Roast peanuts in a 350° F oven for ten minutes and set aside.

2. In a heavy bottom deep saucepan, bring the sugar, corn syrup, water, and butter to a boil until it reaches the hard crack stage of 300° F.

3. Remove from heat and add vanilla, soda and nuts. Mixture will bubble up. Stir well until all is mixed and coated.

4. Spread onto cookie sheet that has been very lightly greased with butter.

5. Let cool and then crack into bite sized shapes.

Exotic Nut Brittle

1 recipe peanut brittle page 171.

1. Make the peanut brittle recipe as normal except that the nuts will be different.

2. Substitute the nuts with brazil nuts, cashews, or almonds.

3. Cook as usual.

Cranberry Maple Syrup

What a treat to start the morning on a cold winter's day. After filling up with hot cereal, head out for a day of cross country skiing or maybe some dog sledding.

1 cup	corn or maple syrup
1 cup	cranberry sauce or crushed berries
1/8 tsp.	cinnamon

1. Mix all of the ingredients until smooth.

Slightly heat cereal before serving if using for pancakes, waffles or breakfast cakes.

Harvest Time Applesauce

Apple picking is a fall tradition and livelihood for many New Brunswickers.

It's easy to get carried away and to arrive home with more apples then you can eat. After visiting one of our many U-pick orchards, applesauce is the perfect answer.

5 lbs.	apples cored, peeled & chopped up
1/2 cup	water
1/2 tsp.	cinnamon
dash	nutmeg

1. Place all in a pot and stir well.

2. Cover and cook on low heat for 1 hour stirring often.

3. Serve warm in a bowl with whipped cream for dessert.

4. Serve by itself or as a condiment with or over lamb or pork dishes, or a hot breakfast cereal. It also makes a great topping for ice cream.

Variation: Add some other fruit such as pears, plums, peaches, blueberries, apricots or cranberries.

Healthy Peanut Butter Cookies

Pack these in your knapsack for a hike along the Fundy Trail.

3/4 cup	peanut butter
1/4 cup	soft butter or margarine
3/4 cup	brown sugar
1	egg
3/4 cup	bran flakes crushed or any crispy cereal
3/4 cup	flour
1/2 tsp.	baking soda

1. Cream peanut butter, butter, sugar and egg together.

2. Add all of the rest of ingredients, mix well.

3. Roll into balls. Press onto cookie sheet with fork.

4. Bake at 375° F for exactly 9 minutes. If you cook longer cookies will be hard.

5. Cool on wire rack.

Variation: Dip half of each cookie in melted chocolate chips.

* * *

Sackville is the quintessential small town with its lovely old homes and tree lined streets. Mount Allison University's beautiful campus is a wonderful place to go for a stroll or for a more natural setting, visit the Sackville Waterfowl Park. The Tantramar marshes combine with geographical location on the flight plan of many migratory birds make this an excellent place to observe an abundance of waterfowl and birds.

Mom's Brownies

3/4 cup	white flour
1 cup	white sugar
1/3 cup	cocoa
1/4 tsp.	salt
1/2 cup	melted shortening
2	eggs
3 tbsp.	cold water
1 tsp.	vanilla

1. In a deep bowl, mix flour, sugar, cocoa, and salt until evenly mixed.

2. Add the rest of the ingredients and beat until smooth.

3. Bake for 30 minutes at 350° F in a non greased pan until brownies start to come away from edge of pan.

4. Let cool and frost if desired.

Sautéed Banana Flambé

1 ripe banana	per person
2 tbsp.	cold water
1 tbsp.	brown sugar
1/4 cup	cherry juice
1 tsp.	minced cherries
1/2 tsp.	black peppercorns
1 tbsp.	butter
2 tbsp.	whipping cream
2 tbsp.	cranberry sauce
dash	cinnamon
1	clove
1 tbsp.	liqueur
1 cup	berries for garnish*

1. Slice banana in half lengthwise, set aside.

2. In a non stick frying pan place all of the above ingredients except the banana and liqueur.

3. Over medium heat mix all well until smooth.

4. Place banana into pan and cook both sides for 2 minutes over medium heat.

5. Add 1 tsp. of liqueur of choice. Carefully add flame if desired and then cover immediately to extinguish.

6. Remove banana and place onto dessert plate.

7. Strain liquid (discarding solid matter) and pour a little over each banana and serve with ice cream or whipping cream.

* Garnish with fresh berries.

Dream Cookies

Base:

1-1/2 cups	graham wafer crumbs*
1 tbsp.	white sugar
1/2 cup	melted butter

1. Mix graham crumbs with sugar and stir until even. Add melted butter and mix until sticky.

2. Press into a 9" x 13" baking dish.

2 cups	milk chocolate, chocolate chips
1 cup	long sweetened coconut
1 cup	nuts of choice
1 cup	sweetened condensed milk

3. Layer the rest of the ingredients, chocolate chips, coconut, nuts and then the cream.

4. Bake for 20 minutes for 350° F. Let cool and cut.

*Shortbread may be used instead of graham crust.

* * *

Fredericton is the capital of New Brunswick. It is also the home of the University of New Brunswick and the oldest university in Canada, Kings College. The original structure is now called the Old Arts Building.

Criss Cross Coconut Squares

1 cup	butter or margarine melted
2	eggs beaten
2 cups	white sugar
1-1/3 cups	flour
1 tsp.	baking powder
1/4 cup	cocoa
1/2 cup	chopped nuts or 1/2 cup coconut
1 cup	coconut
1 tsp.	extract, rum, almond or cherry

1. Mix the butter, eggs, sugar and flour together until smooth.

2. Divide into two even portions. In one part add cocoa, 1/2 cup nuts or coconut and mix well. Set aside. In the other half of mixture add 1 cup of coconut and extract if using. Mix well and set aside.

3. In a lightly greased 8" x 8" baking dish, layer the chocolate mixture in the bottom of the pan and then layer the coconut mixture on top.

4. Bake at 350° F for 25 minutes or until top is golden brown.

Chocolate Rice Crispy Squares

1/2 cup	butter or margarine
1 cup	peanut butter
1 cup	icing sugar
2 cups	rice crispies
1 cup	chocolate chips

1. In a medium, deep pot, melt butter with chocolate chips and then add the peanut butter. Stir until melted.

2. Add icing sugar and remove from heat. Stir well and add rice crispies. Mix until all the rice crispies are coated.

3. Spread into a lightly greased 9" x 13" pan.

4. Frost with 1 cup of any flavor of chocolate chips melted in a microwave and spread it over top of cookies if desired.

Classic Banana Bread

1/4 cup	butter or margarine
2 tbsps.	peanut butter (optional)
1 cup	white sugar
1	egg
3	bananas mashed
1-1/2 cups	white flour
1 tsp.	baking soda
1/2 tsp.	salt

1. Grease a loaf pan. To prevent formation of a thick crust, line the pan with brown paper and then waxed, parchment paper or tinfoil. Set aside.

2. Cream sugar and butter well. Add egg and cream again.

3. Add bananas and mix well.

4. Add dry ingredients and stir until mixture is smooth.

5. Place in loaf pan and bake at 350ºF for 1 hour or until cake tester comes out clean.

6. If top of the bread is getting too dark, gently lay a piece of tinfoil over the top of the pan.

* * *

Hartland in Carleton County boasts the longest covered bridge in the world. Built in 1901 , it is 1282 feet/390 metres long. New Brunswick has many covered bridges but their number is dwindling. Fortunately their historical value and romantic appeal have led to efforts to preserve those that remain.

Peanut Butter Balls

1 cup	peanut butter
2 tbsp.	butter melted
1 tsp.	vanilla
1-1/4 cups	rice crispies
1 cup	icing sugar
3 - 4 tbsp.	water
2 - 3 cups	* long shredded sweetened coconut
* Optional: melted chocolate and/or crushed nuts	

1. Place peanut butter, rice crispies, vanilla and butter in a bowl, stir well. Mixture will be wet.

2. Roll into balls. Set aside in the refrigerator.

3. Mix the icing sugar with the water to make a dipping glaze but not too thin, dip a ball in the glaze and then roll in coconut until covered.

4. Place back in refrigerator to harden.

5. Dip in melted chocolate if desired or roll the balls in crushed peanuts instead of the coconut or use a combination of both.

Golden Graham Bars

1 box	graham wafer squares
1 cup	brown sugar
1/2 cup	milk
1/2 cup	butter
1	egg beaten

1. In a pot over medium heat mix the sugar, milk, egg, and butter, until the sugar has melted and egg is blended.

2. Add 1-1/4 cups of crushed graham wafer crumbs. Mix until all absorbed. Set aside.

3. Line a 9" x 13" pan with graham wafer squares cut to fit the pan exactly. Spread mixture over wafer layer in pan.

4. Place another layer of graham wafers squares on top.

Frosting:

1 cup	chocolate chips
1 tbsp.	peanut butter

1. In the microwave, melt the chocolate chips and peanut butter and stir until smooth.

2. Spread over top of graham wafer squares.

3. Let cool before cutting.

Classic Chocolate Chip Cookies

3/4 cup	brown sugar
1/2 cup	white sugar
1 cup	butter or margarine
1-1/2 tsp.	vanilla
1	egg
1 tsp.	baking soda
1/2 tsp.	salt
1-3/4 cups	flour
1 cup	chocolate chips

1. Combine sugars with butter, egg and vanilla. Blend well.

2. Sift all dry ingredients and add to wet mixture. Mix until all is combined.

3. Add chocolate chips and mix well.

4. Drop with tablespoon onto a greased cookie sheet. Bake at 350° F for 7-15 minutes.

* * *

In its' youth, New Brunswick's economy was almost entirely resource based. World travel relied on wind, wood, and sails. During the 19th century New Brunswick built sailing ships that were world famous, including the Marco Polo.

Low Fat Brownies

1 cup	white sugar
1/3 cup	butter or margarine
1 tsp.	vanilla
3 egg whites	lightly beaten
2/3 cup	flour
1/2 cup	cocoa
1/2 tsp.	baking powder
1/4 tsp.	salt

Glaze for top of brownies

2/3 cup	icing sugar
2 tbsp.	cocoa
1/4 tsp.	vanilla
3-4 tsp.	hot water

1. Cream sugar, butter, eggs and vanilla and mix well.

2. Add the rest of the ingredients. Mix well.

3. Spread into a greased 9" x 13" pan and bake at 350° F for 20 -25 minutes. Let cool.

4. Mix all the ingredients for the glaze together at a quick pace and then spread over cooled brownies. Let stand for 15 minutes to set.

Cut and serve.

Perfect Shortbread

1 cup	butter or margarine or half & half
1/2 cup	icing sugar
1 tsp.	vanilla
2 cups	flour

1. Cream the butter, sugar and vanilla. Add flour and mix until all flour is absorbed. Mixture will be crumbly.

2. Knead dough into 1" balls.

3. Press balls with a fork onto an ungreased cookie sheet.

4. Bake at 300° F for 25 minutes or until bottoms just start to turn lightly golden. Use a doubled cookie sheet to prevent burning.

Peanut Butter Chew Chews

1 cup	peanut butter
1/2 cup	corn syrup
1/2 cup	brown sugar
1 tsp.	vanilla
4 cups	rice crispies cereal

1. Melt all of the above ingredients except for the rice crispies in a pot over medium heat. Stir until mixture is smooth.

2. Remove from heat and add the rice crispies. Stir till all is coated.

3. Spread into a greased 9" x 13" pan. Press firmly to shape.

Let cool.

*Optional: Melt 1 cup of chocolate chips in the microwave for frosting.

Coconut Dream Drops

1 cup	sweetened condensed milk
3 cups	coconut (long sweetened)
1	egg white beaten for 2 minutes
1 tsp.	vanilla
1 tsp.	extract, rum, almond, mint, orange, etc.
1 cup	chocolate chunks or cherries*

1. Mix all well until the coconut is coated well. Add extract if using.

2. Drop by a teaspoon onto a lightly greased cookie sheet and bake at 325° F until coconut turns golden brown.

3. Place a cherry or a wedge of chocolate on top of each cookie.

4. Let the cookies cool slightly before removing from cookie sheet.

5. Cool and store in dry container.

*Optional: For an added flare add 1/2 cup minced dried fruit like apricots or cranberries into the batter before baking.

Irish Soda Bread

2 cups	flour
1 tsp.	baking powder
3 tbsps.	butter
1/2 tsp.	salt
1 tbsp.	sugar

1. In a deep bowl place all of the dry ingredients and stir so they are well mixed.

2. Add butter and rub butter in until mixture is lumpy and crumbly.

3. Add ice cold water, enough to stick together into a rough dough. About 1/4 to 3/4 of a cup, it will depend on the temperature of the room you are in and of your hands.

4. Drape this dough over your roast beef, lamb, or pork.

5. Bake uncovered for 25 minutes on 400° F until just slightly browned.

Hint: This is a great replacement for or addition to potatoes and goes well with gravy.

* * *

Irish immigrants swelled the population of New Brunswick in the 1800's. Descendants of these people are proud of their Irish roots. Each summer they gather to celebrate their heritage at the Irish Festival in the City of Miramichi. The festival is held in July and allows one and all to soak up the music, food and culture of our Irish settlers.

Delicious Chocolate Glaze

1/2 cup	whipping cream
4 squares	semi sweet chocolate (chopped up)
1/2 tsp. extra	e.g. rum, coconut, cherry, mint, etc.
1 tbsp.	peanut butter

1. Bring the whipping cream to a boil in a double boiler over low to medium heat.

2. Add the chocolate, stirring until smooth.

3. When the chocolate is 2/3rd melted, spread over a favorite dessert such as cup-cakes, cakes, cheesecakes, ice-cream, peanut butter cookies, peanut brittle, etc.

Brown Sugar Topping

This sweet, crispy topping is delicious served over apple sauce, fruit salad, trifle or ice cream.

1/4 cup	brown sugar
1/4 cup	rolled minute oats
1 tbsp.	butter (soft)
1/2 cup	white all purpose flour

1. Mix all dry ingredients well and then add butter. Rub butter into flour mixture until even. Bake at 350° F for 10 minutes alone.

Hint: Spread the uncooked mixture over top of an unbaked banana bread. Cut through the top layer with a knife and bake as usual. You can also use it in a salad of greens in place of croutons.

Harvest Time Rhubarb Delight

3 cups	rhubarb diced
1 pkg.	strawberry Jell-O powder
3/4 cup	white sugar
1 pkg.	white or golden commercial cake mix
1-1/4 cup	water

1. Layer in a shallow 9" square baking dish, the above ingredients as follows: cake mix, white sugar, Jell-O powder, rhubarb and the water.

2. Cut mixture with a knife, 12 times in the pattern of a letter x.

3. Bake at 350° F for 40 minutes.

4. Serve piping hot with ice cream, sherbet, or whipped cream drizzled with caramel sauce on page 166.

Fresh Pear and Apple Filo Rounds

Fruit center mixture

2 pears	peeled and sliced
2 apples	peeled and sliced
1/2 tsp.	cinnamon
1/4 cup	water
20 sheets	filo pastry
1/4 cup	melted butter

Crumble mixture

1 cup	oatmeal (minute oats)
1 cup	flour
3/4 cup	brown sugar
1/2 cup	butter (softened)

1. In a medium pot, cook the pear, apple, cinnamon and water. Simmer for 20 minutes on low. Set aside.
2. In a deep mixing bowl, add oatmeal, flour, brown sugar and mix roughly by hand for 2 minutes so all is mixed evenly. Rub in softened butter until mixture turns into a rough lumpy dough. Make sure that all the flour is incorporated. If mixture is too sticky add a little more flour.
3. Lay two sheets of Filo pastry on a cookie sheet. Push the edges toward the center to form a flat circle shape 3 inches in diameter. Make ten Filo circles on the cookie sheet spaced evenly apart .
4. Place 2 tbsps. of fruit mixture in the center of each pastry and top with 2 tbsps. of crumble mixture. Brush exposed edges of pastry with melted butter. Bake at 400° F for 10-15 minutes till filo is crispy and golden brown.
5. Serve piping hot with whipped cream, ice cream on top, or drizzle with maple syrup.

Best Blueberry Grunt

1 recipe	dough boy page 76.
4 cups	blueberries cleaned *
1/4 cup	water
1 tbsp.	lemon juice
1/4 cup	white or brown sugar

1. Place all of the above into a medium sized pot, cover and cook slowly over low heat till it is almost jam. (About 45 minutes).

2. Drop the dumplings into the jam. Push them about half way under the jam. Cover the pot, cook on low heat for 15 minutes. Serve the dumpling with some of the jam sauce and whipped cream, or ice-cream, Sorbet, custard or tapioca spooned over top.

*For variety try using a different fruit like strawberries, raspberries, plums, cranberries etc.

* * *

Pennfield, located between Saint John and St. Stephen, is the home to bountiful blueberry fields. U-picks offer the chance to hand select berries for your favorite recipe.

Best Blueberry Muffins

The key to making these muffins is the flour that coats the blueberries. It prevents them from sinking to the bottom.

1 cup	white sugar
1 cup	blueberries cleaned*
1/2 cup	milk slightly warmed
3 tbsp.	melted butter
2	eggs
2 tsp.	baking powder
1 tsp.	vanilla
1-1/2 cups plus 2 tbsp.	flour
Dash of salt.	

1. Place berries in a bowl by themselves and add 2 tbsps. of flour. Stir gently until all flour is absorbed. Be careful not to crush the berries.

2. Mix all of the ingredients except the berries in a deep mixing bowl until dough is even and smooth. It takes about 7 minutes by hand or 4 with electric mixer. Gently fold in the blueberries.

3. Bake at 375° F for 35-50 minutes or until top of cake springs back or cake tester is clear.

*Cranberries, pineapple, apple, strawberries, etc, may be used in place of or in combination with the blueberries.

Mile High Strawberry Shortcake

4 cups	cleaned strawberries *
1/2 cup	maraschino cherry juice
1/4 cup	whipping cream
1 recipe	white cake page 167 (cooked and cooled)
1 cup	sweetened condensed milk
1 cup	cream whipped
1/2 cup	icing sugar

1. Take 2 cups of the berries and chop lightly, add sweetened condensed milk. Stir and place in air tight container overnight in the fridge.

2. Slice the remaining 2 cups of berries and set aside.

3. Fold icing sugar into whipping cream and beat until stiff peaked. Set aside.

4. Take cake and cut it in half, scoop out the center of the bottom half so as to make a bowl.

5. Place 1 cup of the berry-milk mixture into the hole you created in the bottom layer. Add 1 cup sliced berries on top.

6. Spread the whipping cream mixture over top of the berries. Replace the top half of the cake.

7. Using the last 2 cups of berries, spread all over cake and around the side for decoration.

8. Serve with whipped cream or ice cream.

* Try mixing the fruit, like strawberries & raspberries, crushed cranberry jelly & raspberries, blueberries, etc.

Great Blueberry Cake

3 cups	blueberries
1 recipe	white cake page 167, unbaked.
1 cup	brown sugar
2 tbsps.	white flour
1 cup	cranberry jelly (whole berries crushed)
2 cups	whipped cream
1 recipe	crumble mixture ingredients page 192
Dash of cinnamon.	

1. Make white cake recipe and set aside.

2. Place 2 cups of blueberries into a bowl. Add 2 tbsps. of white flour and coat gently.

3. Fold berries into cake batter very gently. Set aside.

4. Pour into a lightly greased and floured 9" x 9" pan.

5. Make crumble mixture on page 192, and sprinkle over top of cake. Cut through with a knife.

6. Bake at 350° F for 35 minutes or until cake pulls away from edge of pan.

7. While cake is cooking make a jam with 1 cup of blueberries, brown sugar, cinnamon, cranberry jelly and simmer over low heat in a small pot for the same length of time the cake cooks for.

Serve cake with the jam on top followed by whipped cream.

Tea Time Fruited Crumble

3 cups	white flour
6 cups	oatmeal
2-1/2 cups	margarine (softened)
3 cups	brown sugar
2 cups	semi cooked fruit
Dash of cinnamon.	

1. Mix all dry ingredients well, and then rub in butter. Mix till crumbly, and all butter is absorbed. Place half of the mixture in the bottom of an ungreased 9" x 13" pan. Press firmly but do not pack it down. Set aside.

2. For the fruit mixture in the center you can add just about any type of fruit. Use fruit that has been partially cooked in a bit of water. Try using blueberry, apple and blueberry, apple and cranberry, raspberry and cranberry, apple and strawberry, cranberry and strawberry, apple and pear, date and pear, date, apple, strawberry, rhubarb,...etc.

3. Add the top layer of the crumb mixture loosely.

4. Bake at 350° F for 35-50 minutes until the top is golden brown.

5. Serve hot, with a scoop of maple ice cream.

Variation: For date squares make the fruit mixture out of 3 cups of chopped dates and 1 cup of water boiled about 20 minutes until a thick jam is produced. Place between the crumble layers and bake as usual.

Mulled Cider

4 cups	apple juice (fresh or cider variety)
1 tsp.	cinnamon
1 tsp.	allspice
1/2 cup	brown sugar

1. Place the above ingredients into a deep pot and bring to a boil.

2. Reduce heat to low. Serve hot.

3. Serve in a cinnamon sugar rimmed glass, or with a dash of spiced rum.

Conversion Chart

1 tsp. = 5 ml

1 tbsp. = 15 ml

1/4 cup = 50 ml or 2 oz

1/3 cup = 75 ml

1/2 cup = 125 ml or 4oz

2/3 cup = 150 ml

3/4 cup = 175 ml

1 cup = 250 ml or 8oz

1lb = 454g

1000 ml = 1 litre or 4 cups

1 kg = 2.2 lbs

30 ml = 1 oz

1/4 tsp. = 1 ml

8 oz = 1 cup

16 oz = 1 lb

About the Author

Karen began cooking at home as soon as she was tall enough to reach the counter and discover how fun cooking was. Her love of cooking has taken her from a pizza shop, fruit and vegetable stand to a little French Café.

Now she reserves her cooking for family and friends who love to gather in her typical Maritime Kitchen.

Index

A

B

C

D

E

F

G

H

I

Q

R

S